ENAMELLING ON PRECIOUS METALS

ENAMELLING ON PRECIOUS METALS

Jeanne Werge-Hartley

THE CROWOOD PRESS

First published in 2002 by
The Crowood Press Ltd
Ramsbury, Marlborough
Wiltshire SN8 2HR

British Library Cataloguing-in-Publication Data
A catalogue record for this book is available from the British Library.

ISBN 978 1 84797 205 7

Dedication
Dedicated to my mother, Emily Vauvelle, to whom I owe so much.

Photograph previous page: *Tea Dance teapot. 1998.* Fred Rich.

Disclaimer
Many of the techniques used in enamelling involve hazardous materials and procedures. If all the Health and Safety instructions are adhered to, no problems should arise. The author and publisher accept no liability for any accidents, howsoever caused, to any reader following instructions from the text of the book.

Acknowledgements
I would like to thank all the artist enamellers who appear in this book for their generous response to my request for illustrations and information about their work. I would also like to acknowledge the valuable assistance which I received from the following people:

David Beasley, the Librarian at Goldsmiths' Hall
Catherine Hughes at Goldsmiths' Hall
Sonia and David Newell-Smith at Tadema Gallery
Ken Blundell at J. Blundell & Sons Ltd
Laurence Thomas at Cooksons Precious Metals
Sarah Wilson
Muriel Wilson

Last, but not least, a thank you to my family for their support and to my husband Alan for giving up this summer's sailing for word processing and editing.

Picture Credits
Ruth Ball: pages 22 (bottom left), 115, 117, 120, 121, 122; Alf Barnes: pages 145, 146 (top); Clarissa Bruce: pages 20, 52, 83 (top); Dorothy Cockrell: page 131; Alan Cooper: pages 22 (top), 113, 123; Maureen Carswell: page 15; John Cohen: page 114; Genevieve Cummins: page 80; Joel Degan: pages 65 (bottom), 133, 136 (top), 141 (bottom), 142 (left); Maureen Edgar: page 146 (bottom); Rodney Forte: pages 24, 25, 61, 65 (top), 73, 75 (top), 77, 132, 144; Penny Gildea: page 136 (bottom); Mike Inch: page 140 (bottom); John Jillings: pages 110, 112 (bottom); John Knill: pages 23, 90, 99, 100 (bottom), 107, 108, 109, 135 (bottom); Joan MacKarell: page 135 (top); Sheila McDonald: pages 50 (top), 126, 129, 130; Andrew Metcalf: pages 14 (right), 85, 86, 87, 88, 89, 95, 137 (bottom); Sarah Macrae: pages 19, 26, 27, 28, 30, 31, 34, 45, 49 (top), 50 (bottom), 51 (bottom), 53, 56 (bottom), 70, 92, 93 (top), 93 (bottom), 94 (bottom), 96, 97, 98, 138 (bottom right); David Newell-Smith: pages 10, 11, 12, 13, 18; R.C.A: page 141 (top); Robert Sanderson: pages 14 (left), 55, 78, 79, 81, 83 (bottom); Jane Short: page 82; J A Smith: pages 56 (top), 111, 112 (top); Jeanne Werge-Hartley: pages 7, 8 (bottom), 8 (top), 9, 16, 17, 21, 22 (bottom right), 42, 47, 48, 49 (bottom), 51 (top), 57, 68, 69, 71, 72, 74, 75 (bottom), 91, 94, 100 (top), 101, 116, 124, 125, 127, 128, 137 (top right), 138 (except bottom right), 140 (top), 142 (right), 152, 153, 154, 156, 157, 160; Peter White: pages 53, 54, 62, 63, 104, 137 (top left), 143.

Typefaces used: Plantin (main text and headings).

Typeset and designed by
D & N Publishing
Baydon, Marlborough, Wiltshire.

Printed and bound in Malaysia by Times Offset (M) Sdn. Bhd.

CONTENTS

INTRODUCTION

The aim of this book is to interest all enamellers and perhaps encourage them to try new techniques and ideas beyond the traditional limitations. I felt that it would be valuable not only to investigate the details and alternative methods of each technique but also to pay tribute to the excellent contemporary artist enamellers of Great Britain, so I have deliberately restricted the scope of the book to British enamellers although I am aware of the beautiful work done in other countries. Equally I am aware that I have not been able to mention and illustrate the work of every interesting enameller practising in this country today and for this I apologize. The book had to have limits, so I had to make difficult choices. I selected some artists because they are at the top of their profession, others for their innovative or particular use of a technique and yet others who, in my opinion, have been important in the exciting resurgence of enamelling during the past forty years.

As a very young girl I remember watching my grandfather, Achille Vauvelle, who was an enamel painter of some experience. I realized even at that stage the intense concentration and patience that was required, and the nostalgic image of that quiet and still room, of being allowed to sit and watch as long as I remained silent, is with me still. He painted on metal plaques, glass and china so I inherited many boxes filled with sealed glass tubes of his painting enamels and sample plaques and, having recently been in contact with enamel painters, I am inspired to emulate my grandfather and attempt some enamel painting with his colours.

My National Diploma in Design was taken at Leeds College of Art in a course for jewellery with enamelling at special level. The course did not exist when I enrolled at the college but while exploring the studios during the first few weeks I found a workshop in which a little old man in a long white coat stood hand polishing a gold and opal necklace. It was Mr Barton, the tutor in jewellery. This was it! This I had to do, and I gradually persuaded the hierarchy that they should provide a full-time course for me, which they finally did. I was fortunate to be tutored by Miss Muriel Noble, a dear lady of mature years and one of the Glasgow Girls, who not only introduced me to all the traditional techniques of cloisonné, champlevé, and plique à jour, but encouraged me to experiment and include enamelling in my jewellery for my final exhibition. I was one of a very few students to take the NDD in jewellery and enamelling that year in England and all my examination papers were handwritten.

For my major piece I vividly remember making a cloisonné panel that took many hours of soldering to put all the wires in place, and recollect arriving in college at 7.30 one morning to start grinding and washing the colours, spending the rest of the day laying them in and at about 8 o'clock that evening firing the piece with my heart racing. I knew that if anything went wrong I was back to square one and I would not have time to do it all again. Fortunately it did go well and I still have the piece to prove it.

After leaving college I was appointed the stage jeweller at the Royal Opera House, making theatrical costume jewellery for the ballet and the opera companies, and

Necklace in 9K white and 18K yellow gold, with cloisonné and crystal slice. 1996. Jeanne Werge-Hartley.

attended evening classes at the Central School of Art to continue working with precious metals.

Enamelling was an important element of the jewellery course that I started and led at Portsmouth College of Art from 1957. This developed from part-time classes into a Southern Regional Diploma course and, in 1982, to the first Higher National Diploma (HND) course from which students won awards at a national level. We were able to provide a room dedicated to enamelling from 1977, which enabled the students to be taught the basic enamelling skills; many of them went on to produce exciting pieces. They enjoyed experimenting, joining the enamels with other materials, such as carved ebony, silks, refractory metals and porcelain, while developing interesting techniques to combine them in an innovative way.

Purse in silver, champlevé and silk. Theresa Haskell (student).

necklace – but I hope that my personal notes on techniques and materials, along with the information generously supplied by many specialist enamellers with whom I have been in contact, will be of interest.

A short while ago a jeweller friend, who is not an enameller, gave me a box in the hope that the contents would interest me. Imagine my delight and surprise to find a collection of assorted lump enamel once belonging to Mrs Nelson Dawson and a book written by her in 1906. It was obviously her own copy as the inside page bears her name and the address in Chiswick Mall, where her workshop was situated. The book is entitled *Enamels*, one of the Little Books of Art series and was priced at 2/6 (12.5p). Those who are interested in

ABOVE: Necklace (detail) of Yemeni design in hardenable silver, 18K yellow gold foil and wires, and enamel. 1999. Jeanne Werge-Hartley.

RIGHT: Fob watch and bead chain in silver and enamel. Catherine Kirby (student).

Throughout this time I continued to produce pieces for commission, worked for galleries and exhibitions, undertook research projects (such as that on the use of 1715 silver in relation to enamelling for Johnson Matthey) and, as a founder member of the Designer Jewellers Group, helped to promote the idea of the artist jeweller. From these years of practice in my workshop, of lecturing and contact with other craftsmen I feel that I have acquired a body of knowledge which I would like to pass on. I am not an enamel purist, I use enamel as colour to enhance my jewellery, often to produce a decorative unit inspired by a painting – or by colourful architecture as in my Yemeni

the history of the early artist enamellers will recognize the significance of this find, for this lady was an enameller of some repute at the beginning of the twentieth century.

Edith Dawson had fewer technical aids than are available today but even she was conscious that machines that saved her time could not reproduce the quality of finish that the ancient, laborious, hands-on methods achieved, and wished that craftsmen could afford to spend time reaching for perfection rather than compromising for commercial reasons. In her little book she quotes from *Sea to Sea* by Rudyard Kipling, writing about his visit to an enamel factory in Kyoto:

It may take a month to put a pattern on a plate in outline, another month to fill in the enamel, but the real expenditure of time does not commence till the polishing. A man sits down with the rough article, all his tea things, a tub of water, a flannel, and two or three saucers full of assorted pebbles from the brook. He does not get a wheel with tripoli, or emery, or buff. He rubs for a month, three months or a year. He rubs lovingly, with his soul in his finger-ends, and little by little the efflorescence of the fired enamel gives way and he comes down to the lines of silver, and the pattern in all its glory is there waiting for him.

Earrings in 9K white gold, 18K yellow gold, and enamel. 1997. Jeanne Werge-Hartley.

1 ENAMELLING SINCE THE NINETEENTH CENTURY

The Easter Pendant, an egg-shaped reversible pendant in silver and translucent enamel, by one of Scotland's foremost artists of the Arts and Crafts movement. c.1902. Phoebe Traquair.

Like other arts, enamelling has had its peaks and troughs and in its own way illustrates the trends in fashion of any given time in history. Although still recent in terms of historical interest the last 150 years have seen two distinctive periods that have produced enamelling of great innovative excellence.

The industrial revolution of the early nineteenth century brought about a decline in the creative forces in the arts, in which the function of the artist craftsman was replaced by machinery of mass production to meet the growing demand for consumer goods. In the second half of the century there was a surge of energy which focused on the decorative and applied arts and gave rise to new art movements, which, for the first time since the Renaissance period, also involved the minor crafts such as metalwork and enamelling. In Britain and France many artists and architects turned their attention to the decorative arts and the majority chose to design jewellery and enamels, so much so that they equalled the number of trade-trained jewellers. The work of both groups was of sufficient originality to give them equal status with exhibiting painters and sculptors.

One of the best known was the French jewellery designer and enameller René Lalique, who was apprenticed in 1876 to the renowned Parisian goldsmith Louis Aucoc. This experience with a goldsmith gave Lalique a basic knowledge of materials and techniques, and in 1878 he came to England to attend a School of Art in Sydenham where he devoted his time to drawing from nature. He became an outstanding draughtsman, as can be seen in his jewellery sketches and the designs for his later pieces, and it was this combination of drawing and technical skill that made his work so strong. After two years in England he returned to Paris at the age of twenty and from 1881 spent the next twenty years designing the enamelled jewellery which was to gain him a reputation unmatched by any of his contemporaries. By 1887 he had two workshops employing about thirty craftsmen and by the turn of the century his name was synonymous with the Art Nouveau movement.

While the Art Nouveau style flourished in France, the Arts and Crafts movement with its medieval influences was predominant in Britain. Guilds and craft societies

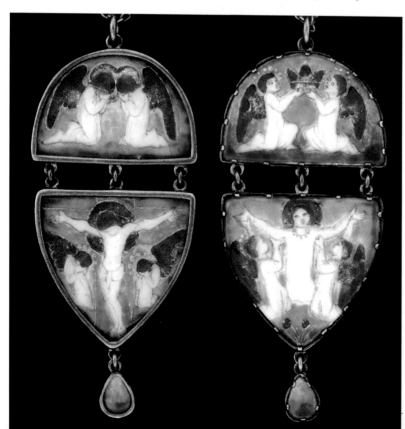

were beginning to form, the first one being the Guild of St George, inspired and set up by the art critic and writer John Ruskin in 1872. The return to hand craftsmanship that William Morris and John Ruskin advocated and promoted so earnestly resulted in the foundation in 1884 of the Art Workers Guild by a group of architect designers including Horsley, Lethaby, Newton, Macartney and Prior, who were all members or former members of Norman Shaw's practice and of the Guild of St George. The original members were joined soon afterwards by an informal group of artists, the 'Fifteen', including Crane, Morris, Mackmurdo, Shaw, Lutyens, Voysey and Ashbee, and by Henry Wilson and J. Paul Cooper, who were to become outstanding craft revival silversmiths and jewellers. Three years later, in 1887, metalworker W.A.S. Benson formed the Arts and Crafts Exhibition Society to show the work of the craftsmen members of the Art Workers Guild, and Walter Crane became its first president. The Exhibition Society still exists today as the Society of Designer Craftsmen and continues to promote exhibitions of the best of British craftsmanship.

FAR LEFT: A jewelled and gold enamelled pendant. c.1908. Henry Wilson.

LEFT: The Snowdrop Pendant, in gold and painted enamel. c.1900. C.R. Ashbee.

The Art Workers Guild, which also still flourishes and has a significant membership of master craftsmen, was formed to advance education in all the visual arts and crafts, and many of its members were not only skilled in arts and crafts but were actively engaged in the great renaissance taking place in the leading art schools. Walter Crane, in particular, was influential in education and held many important positions, including that of Principal of the Royal College of Art in 1898.

A gold necklace with sapphires, diamonds and enamel. c.1905. Mr and Mrs Nelson Dawson.

In 1886 the first enamelling classes were held in Britain. These came about owing to the energy and enthusiasm of Thomas Armstrong, the director of the South Kensington Museum (now the Victoria and Albert Museum) who invited M. Dalpayrat, one of the few painter enamellers of Paris, to give twelve practical demonstrations to twelve students of the National Art Training School (which was founded in 1853 and became the Royal College of Art in 1886). The classes had far-reaching results for, although none of the other students who attended the enamelling demonstrations are known to have continued to enamel, the exception, Alexander Fisher, became one of the most celebrated enamellers of the first part of the twentieth century. His book on enamelling remains one of the most eminent of its kind, and he was a highly influential teacher – he started the courses at the Central School of Arts and Crafts that heralded the revival of enamelling.

One of Fisher's students was Nelson Dawson and the latter taught his wife Edith who, though a perfectionist and very critical of her own work, produced some of the most accomplished enamels of that time. In 1900 the Dawsons had an exhibition of their combined work at the Fine Arts Society in Bond Street. In her book *Enamels* she states that the Dalpayrat classes were the beginning of the revival of enamelling in Britain and goes on to comment that this renewed interest also affected the work that was going on in Paris, giving strength to the revival there.

After M. Dalpayrat's classes there was a period when very little happened, and it was not until *circa* 1901 that facilities for enamelling were offered to students in art schools. One of the schools to which Mrs Dawson gives special mention was Birmingham, where the students were working with 'steady enthusiasm'. In her book she praises the work of Alexander Fisher, George Frampton RA, who introduced enamel into his sculptures, Henry Wilson,

Gold and enamel Jewel. c.1898. George Frampton (sculptor).

the Gaskins and many more who were to establish the revival of the art of enamelling in the 1900s.

Despite all the encouragement and some interesting work being done under the aegis of the Arts and Crafts Exhibition Society, enamelling never gained the following Mrs Dawson had predicted. At the end of her book she comments about enamelling that:

> This above all other arts, if it is to live, must be done well, and with a purpose, a good conscience working with a capable hand and brain, and we may yet have a school of enamels equal to, perhaps even better than, any that the world has ever seen.

Sadly, for many reasons it was not to happen in her lifetime. Two world wars and the apparent decline of the artist enameller delayed her prediction until the last quarter of the twentieth century.

Enamelling survived during the Art Deco period in the jewellery trade, and enamel, usually black or dark blue, was used by the big jewellery houses of Boucheron and Cartier and the jeweller Jean Fouquet to emphasize the hard angular lines of the Deco geometry, with large gemstones providing the colour. Because designers generally were distanced from the craftsmanship, the jewellery of this period appears soulless in comparison to the visionary qualities of Art Nouveau.

A new revival of enamelling in the 1970s stemmed once again from initiatives within the Central School of Arts and Crafts. Patrick Furse was a lecturer in enamelling at the college from 1974 to 1984, having been engaged by the principal, Morris Kesselman, to tutor in the industrial design department and to teach mural painting in the fine art department. Furse was well regarded by many students in the college and it was Brian Wood, at that time head of the jewellery department, who invited him to teach the jewellers. His teaching methods were experimental: he admitted to knowing nothing about jewellery and sought to involve the students in finding out the possibilities of enamel colours. Jane Short remembers that he was not so much concerned about what the students did with enamels as with helping them discover for themselves a personal system of colour that would give them the knowledge to mix and apply the enamels to their work. Although at that time Pat was not a jewellery enameller he certainly gave the students a wonderful introduction to the methodology of using enamels and passed on to both Jane Short and Fred Rich an excitement for the medium, which they both gratefully acknowledge.

Jane Short has tried to communicate this enthusiasm for experimental attitudes in her own work as well as in her teaching. Brian Woods invited Jane back to the Central School to teach after her MA show at the Royal College of Art, and she has taught in many other colleges worldwide, including West Dean College in Sussex, where many well-known enamellers learnt from Jane and gained so much from her skills and passion for enamel. Jane also tutored Fred Rich and Fiona Rae at the Central School. Fred developed the enthusiasm for bright colours first inspired by Pat Furze and, not content with working on a small scale, went on to create

RIGHT: Butterfly Vase, in the collection of the Worshipful Company of Goldsmiths. 1996. Fred Rich.

BELOW: Silver and enamel brooches. 2000. Jane Short.

Copper vessels. 1993.
Maureen Carswell.

large enamelled silver items (*see* Chapter 4). Fiona Rae became interested in enamels as an extension of her love of colour, which is integral to her interest in sculpture. The enamels made by Fiona as a student showed an interesting restraint and delicacy of colour; she designed flower forms that had graduated matt enamel colours, further developing the palette of the enameller at that time. Fiona now teaches at the Central School.

Ros Conway was a student at the Central School from 1970 to 1973 but, although initially interested in enamelling, she did not enjoy the work she was producing at that time. She was fortunate to receive a Crafts Council grant in 1980, which enabled her to study with Jane Short in her workshop for two years. This resulted in a one-man exhibition at the Victoria and Albert Museum in 1982. When a piece of metal is covered with enamel it often appears to be made of glass and this was the aspect that Ros wanted to develop. She contacted Diana Hobson, who was working in pâte de verre, an intriguing method developed in the nineteenth century in France and, despite the very difficult technical problems, Ros fell under the spell of this extraordinary fragile and luminous glass technique (*see* Chapter 7).

By the mid 1970s the influences were there and well established by inspired and inspiring teachers and, as in 1906, part-time classes began to spring up and enamelling at all levels of competence and originality was emerging. Concerns began to be expressed at certain directions being taken in which enamel was being used without much aesthetic consideration and with a lack of sensitivity. However, this is common to all areas of the art and craft world and it is important to realize the value of educating the public in the rigours of professional enamelling and exposing people to the beautiful work of our very best artist enamellers.

When Hans Theilade, who owned the enamel shop Crafts Unlimited in London, transferred his business to Wales, he discovered through a newsletter he circulated to his customers that there was not only an interest in forming a local group of enamellers but a need for a national society. At this point Hans contacted Maureen Carswell, who works in enamel and copper and is a respected craftsman, and together with a small group they assembled a steering committee that resulted in the Guild of Craft Enamellers being formed in 1979. The Guild is open to anyone who is interested in enamels or enamelling, but in order to set goals it was decided to define standards of achievement. Under the chairmanship of Leslie Humpherys a committee was invited to set standards for the selection of Associate Craftsman (AGE); later the level of Craftsman of the Guild of Enamellers (CGE) and Fellow (FGE) were introduced. Additionally, membership with Honours at all three levels can be gained by submission of an academic thesis of sufficient merit on an approved subject. Some of the first selectors were Fred and Phil Barnes, Jeanne Werge-Hartley and John Ball. The Guild has now 286 members, issues a very interesting quarterly journal and holds an informative and educational annual weekend conference. There is a good selection of enamelling books, catalogues and videos available to members.

In 1985 Maureen Carswell went to the Limoges Biennale Internationale and was asked if Britain would be interested in becoming affiliated to an international enamelling association based in Limoges. The British Society of Enamellers was formed to meet the criteria of the Limoges Association and a steering committee representative of all aspects of the craft was formed to discuss and formulate the constitution. It included Maureen Carswell, Alexandra Placzek (Raphael), Edward

Heath, Endre Hevezi, Pat Johnson, Ian Robertson, Ruth Rushby, Jane Short and others. Gudde Jane Skyrme was also on this committee and played a very important part in the running of the Society. Gudde also gave much of her own time and creative energy to setting up the outlet in Camden Mews for enamels and equipment when Hans Theilade decided to supply only schools and colleges.

Maureen Carswell was elected chairman for the first five years with Alexandra Raphael as secretary, and it is through their and Gudde's dedication that the Society has developed into the prestigious exhibiting group that it is today. The first members were invited and then a selection committee was formed as other enamellers joined, first at associate level and then promoted to full membership. In 1986 the membership was only thirty-four, but by 2001 it had more than doubled in size. Since the formation of the Society there have been exhibitions in many venues in Britain including the Electrum Gallery in London and internationally in France, Switzerland, Germany, America and Russia.

In September 1997 six executive members of the Society, Sarah Letts, Joan Mackarell, Alexandra Raphael, Gudde

Studio Fusion interior.

Development drawings for a Yemeni necklace. Jeanne Werge-Hartley.

Jane Skyrme, Elizabeth Turrell and Tamar de Vries Winter, having seen and being enthused by a gallery devoted to enamelling in Barcelona, took the decision to find a site in London where they could open a gallery. It was about the time that the Oxo Tower Wharf on the South Bank was being developed into a new and exciting series of small and very individual outlets and workshops, and the enamellers quickly negotiated for a position on the first floor riverside and opened the gallery in December 1996. It is an appropriate setting for the first, and as yet only, gallery in Britain to be dedicated to enamels: the area is light, the elegant glass showcases present the work clearly and the view across the river to the City through a floor-to-ceiling glass wall makes an inspiring backcloth. The name of the gallery is simply Studio Fusion, an apt and descriptive title. Work from the six co-directors, from invited established artist enamellers and from promising recent art college graduates combines to create an exciting and diverse collection. It is stunningly beautiful!

A striking comparison can be made not far away, in Islington, where the Tadema Gallery has the most wonderful collection of enamelled pieces by the Nelson Dawsons, the Gaskins, Ashbee and others of the end of the nineteenth century, and it is interesting to speculate how many of the lovely pieces in Studio Fusion will become treasures in a similar gallery to the Tadema Gallery in a hundred years' time.

DESIGNING

Drawing is a necessary tool to externalize and develop ideas and to help carry them through to a working design result. To understand, appreciate and see shape, form, proportion, and colour is not an

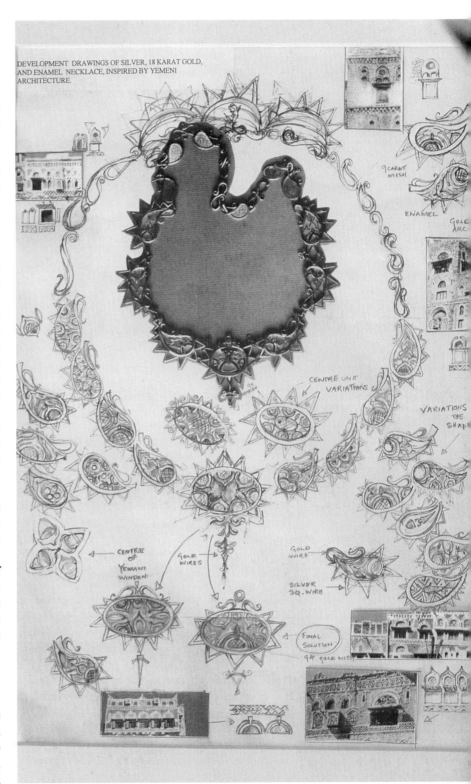

DEVELOPMENT DRAWINGS OF SILVER, 18 KARAT GOLD, AND ENAMEL NECKLACE, INSPIRED BY YEMENI ARCHITECTURE.

inborn ability, although some artists and artist craftsmen do have an instinctive and innate sense of those things. Most people have to be taught how to look and see and apply that knowledge to their drawing, and how to develop an awareness through continual visual recording, assessment and self-criticism.

Designing is a reaction to a stimulus which can have many starting points. A client-imposed brief, self-imposed constraints, or the limitations of a specific technique may steer the designer's thinking towards a specific solution. The design may result in one piece or in a collection of work. Sometimes a topic title is presented as a theme for an exhibition and this is often an inspirational impetus to a designer to initiate a new series of design concepts or may even give rise to a total change of direction.

Designing should be a continuous progression, starting with the identification of the problem, moving through numerous stages of investigation, research, notation, maturation, visual recording and analysis, until a satisfactory conclusion has been reached. At any point during this process the intuitive leap to a conclusion – known as inspiration – may occur but it is not something to expect or to wait for, it is a bonus. A good designer will have ideas that can be stored for future use surfacing through the subconscious at both appropriate and inappropriate moments and should instantly note them in some permanent record.

In the course at Portsmouth it was obvious that the students' ability to record and make marks improved rapidly when they were asked to make 'visual records', a much less intimidating title than drawing. As the weeks passed they became so involved in the mix of words and graphic marks that recorded their ideas in a milieu that concentrated on what they were trying to express rather than the style of the expression, that their drawing gradually improved, they became more confident and, with encouragement, they suddenly found they were enjoying the process. As they improved so they drew more and the upward spiral of practice and graphic fluency began.

Many students in colleges today are relying on computers as aids to design, and are losing by neglect the process of drawing by hand. Although there is no doubt that computer-aided design (CAD) is a very useful tool and excellent value as another technique to acquire, the direct link between the brain of a designer and a flexible and inspirational drawing tool making marks on paper can never be replaced.

Designing is indivisible from the making process, and a profound understanding of the skills in a craft informs good design. It is only when a craftsman has become practised and confident in the chosen area, be it jewellery, enamelling or anything else, that the ability is developed to reach through the mechanics and the constraints of the technique and achieve the aesthetics and beauty of the work. At that point the maker can then truly be called an artist craftsman.

2 ENAMELS

DEFINITION OF ENAMEL

The basic medium of enamel is a clear flux or frit, composed of materials such as flint, sand, potash, soda and lead, which is coloured by the addition of various metallic oxides in powder form. This mix gives a comparatively soft glass that has a firing temperature between 750°C and 800°C (1382–1472°F). Each oxide helps to create the various colours depending on the quantity used and can be modified by the addition of other oxides. A transparent cobalt blue is manufactured by adding black oxide of cobalt to powdered flint glass, and oxides of copper will result in various shades and tones of green from pale aquamarine to rich emerald. The brilliant and beautiful reds are generally more expensive than other colours because gold oxide is used in most opaque and transparent red enamels. Soft greys are made with platinum oxides, while uranium and antimony are used in yellows, tin in white and iridium in rich blacks.

Opalescent enamels are made in the same way but with the addition of tin oxide, which creates the opacity.

TYPES OF ENAMEL

Transparent Enamels

These enamels allow light and colour to pass through to the metallic surface on which they are laid. They are used over a patterned, engraved or carved surface to great effect, as in Jane Short's Millennium Plate (*see* page 20). Light transparent colours can be used for plique à jour but their main use is in cloisonné, basse taille and occasionally champlevé. When using standard silver many of the colours need to have an under layer of flux, but when enamelling over fine silver, hardenable silver, most of the gold alloys and pure gold, many colours can be placed directly on to the metal. Red enamels nearly always need a prior fluxing except on pure gold, 18K gold and platinum. Like pink enamels they need only to be fired once for a beautiful colour – a

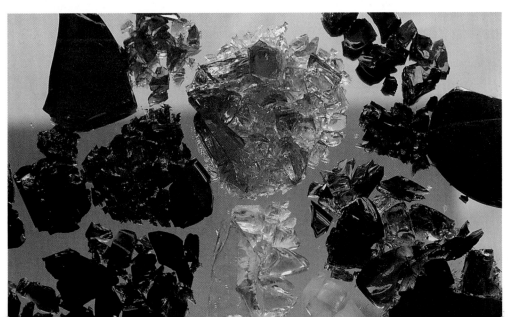

Lump enamel (originally belonging to Mrs Nelson Edith Dawson).

Millennium Plate in engraved silver and champlevé, in the collection of the Worshipful Company of Goldsmiths. Jane Short.

Millennium Plate (detail).

> **Melting Points**
>
> Although some enamel colours are able to withstand great heat and for some colours the higher the temperature the lovelier the result will be, it is prudent to remember the melting temperature of the metal to which it is being fused.

second firing will produce brown and orange colours. Transparent enamels need to be washed very diligently but should not be ground too finely (50–60 mesh), as the coarser ground enamels fire to a clearer transparency, particularly the reds.

Opaque Enamels

These enamels allow no light through at all, so the light bounces back from the surface. They are manufactured by inert crystalline particles being added to the raw glass, grown inside the enamel in the process of smelting or cooling, or once the enamel is reheated during a kiln firing. Pre-ground enamels work well with opaque colours but the washing process must still be stringent in order to achieve clean and problem-free colours and smooth-fired, bubble-free surfaces. Opaque enamels are used mainly in the champlevé techniques, including heraldic and civic regalia. Opaques can also

be very attractive in cloisonné and, as long as the firing temperatures are comparable, they can be fired alongside contrasting transparent colours. If opaque enamels start to appear dull it usually indicates that they have been subjected to an overlong stay in the kiln at too low a temperature. It could also mean that they have been put into acid or pickle, or that the enamel was underwashed or just old. Both black and white enamels can have problems. Black should have only one firing as it does not like acid; it can be tricky to get a spotless and perfect black. White enamel may go yellow at the edges if fired at too high a temperature. A good red opaque can be achieved over silver by applying a thin layer of flux first, but it is almost impossible to avoid a black edge.

Opalescent Enamels

Like opal gemstones these enamels have a surface in which there are colour changes. These are caused by the different refractive indices of the matrix glass and the crystals. The opalescence, which can be compared with the glaze on high-quality china, is produced by preparing the enamel with droplets smaller than the wavelength of light, which are not capable of mixing together. The range of opal colours is limited to white, red, pink, mauve and

Brooch with opaque enamel and ebony inlay. Sophie Taylor (student).

blue. The colours across the surface of the enamel are subtle and range from a milky white to elusive and beguiling hues. Opalescent enamels need to be fired twice. The first firing should be very high until the enamel is transparent; the piece should then be cooled and fired again at a lower temperature. It can be removed from the kiln to assess the opalescence and refired until the piece reaches the required effect. Opal colours do not need flux under them except on fine silver. Often these opal colours can be fired over opaque enamels to achieve a marble-like effect.

Grisaille Enamels

Grisaille enamel is a very finely ground white powder (325–400 mesh) and is used for building up a graduated white design on a dark background. Soyer Limoges White is recommended and usually a dark blue or black enamel is used for the background. The effect is very similar to a cameo. The white enamel is prepared on a piece of glass with a horn spatula. It is

mixed, or triturated, with small amounts of oil of turpentine, which will make a thick paste, after which different thinners may be added to give different effects. Adding turpentine will give sharp lines and curves as the paste does not flow as it does when mixed with oil of lavender, which allows the white to flow from the solid paste to delicate shadings that blend into the background without a sharp contour. Using only plain distilled water gives a much more varied range, from dense opaque white to the finest veil-like transparency, but each brushstroke leaves a small, delicate but solid rim (*see* Chapter 7).

Painted and Limoges Enamels

The enamels used for painting are even more finely ground than the white enamel used for grisaille. They should be stored in airtight containers and only a small amount prepared for each day's work. The enamel powder is prepared on porcelain or on a square of glass and triturated with a steel palette knife with a variety of essences or essential oils. There are contemporary mediums made of synthetic or organic mixes, but the traditional oils such as oil of lavender or oil of turpentine are used by the majority of professionals. Kenneth Bates in his book, *Enamelling*, suggests oil of sassafras, which is derived from a North American tree of the laurel family. It is a volatile, aromatic oil that carries a risk of toxicity and skin irritation, so care should be taken when using it.

RIGHT: Mr and Mrs Cameron in painted enamel. Gillie Hoyte Byrom.

BELOW: Earrings in silver and painted enamel. Ruth Ball.

BELOW RIGHT: Painted enamel. Dayna White.

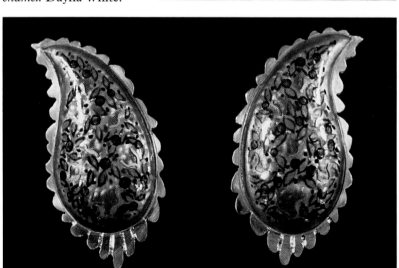

ENAMEL COLOURS

Although most enamels can be bought pre-ground in a powder form ready for use, many professional enamellers prefer to buy their colours in lump form and go through the process of grinding and washing the enamels themselves. The range of colours is enormous and, even then, each one of these colours will be modified by both the metal it is covering, and by the use of a different transparent colour laid over the first fired enamel. Many enamellers have their own range of preferred colours and manufacturers and have a reasonable understanding of how these colours will behave in specific firing circumstances and their likely reaction with different metals. However, there are still uncertainties and variables and most enamellers agree that there is an element of risk which must be built into the expectations of the finished piece.

Red and Pinks

True reds and pinks are particularly difficult to achieve on precious metals. High karat golds (in particular the 18K white golds) and platinum usually give the best results, but all colours react differently, and experience and trials are the only ways to generate confidence in achieving true colours. When enamelling red on silver the metal must be perfectly clean and free of firestain, firescale and grease. Phil Barnes uses a Schauer No 8 enamel on silver and swears by it and Sarah Wilson has used the new Kujaku reds with great success. It is necessary to fire reds high, fast and only once, but Sarah in her technical notes about the Kujaku enamels observes that on her autumnal silver vessel, where the firings were slower and repeated because of the thicker gauge of silver, the red (105A) remained clear and bright.

Pure pinks are difficult to achieve and need a flux beneath them; often a salmon or orange pink are the nearest colours possible. Phil Barnes thinks that certain pure mauves (and he mentions Schauer No 27) are a good substitute to give a pink directly onto silver. Opaque reds and pinks are best laid onto a thin layer of white enamel. A perfect transparent red can be fired on any metal if a piece of gold foil, or very thin high-karat sheet gold, is secured between the metal and the red enamel. Benevenuto Cellini recommended that the best way to obtain translucent red on gold was to cool the surface with bellows as soon as it came out of the furnace. There are some other comments on red enamels in the manufacturers' tables.

Pure silver brooches decorated with gold wire, gold foil, cloisonné and pink tourmaline. 2001. Alexandra Raphael.

Sarah Wilson's Colours

Some colour names are fascinating and conjure up potent visual impressions, such as Madonna blue, dark sea blue, bishop's purple and redcurrant. Often enamellers use these names, or their stock numbers, when describing things they have seen to other enamellers. A piece that Sarah Wilson wrote in the *Society of British Enamellers Newsletter* some years ago sums this up very clearly:

This beautiful salmon pink (used without flux) was the only way to describe a striking sunset over the rooftops of Clapham which also had streaks of Schauer No 8 and deepened into rich Schauer 6080 as the darkness fell. Phil (Barnes) understood me completely, but then he is a chronic sufferer too ...

Throughout the day, our conversations of colours are peppered with references to porridge fading into slate (pale mauve graded with pale violet blue), anthracite (deep gunmetal grey), oranges which can be pink without flux or light red laid thinly, cornflower which we call electric blue, but on the jar it's stored in, [it] has only the bland title tr. blue 6073 (not to be confused with bl.3076 though).

Sarah recently took over the outlet for supplies of enamel and enamelling equipment that was started by enameller Gudde Skyrme at Camden Mews in London. The outlet is now in Clapham and called Vitrum Signum. The enamel stocklist is very comprehensive and Sarah estimates that she has a range of approximately

Vases in engraved silver and champlevé (Three Seasons). 2001. Sarah Wilson.

800 enamels in stock and twelve fluxes for gold and silver. Her obvious delight in colour makes her a special person with whom to discuss enamels, and her knowledge of the different characteristics of her stock is invaluable. In her own work she tends to use very soft and muted hues and she thinks that this is a reaction to being surrounded by so many vivid colours. Sarah is very generous about passing on any results from her own trials of new enamels to other enamellers; for instance her information sheet on Japanese Kujaku reds, where her tests are not only detailed but delightfully personal as well. Sarah has kindly given permission to include the lists of the enamels she stocks with all the relevant detail of firing temperatures (*see* Technical Information).

Thompson Enamels

Craftsmen who have been involved with enamels for a number of years were disappointed when it became impossible to acquire Thompson enamels from the USA. This was due to changes in the US health and safety laws, which stopped Thompsons using lead in their enamels. The Thompson colours were superb and are missed by all who used them. There has been a considerable amount of work done to match those colours to lead-based British, Japanese and French enamels, but out of roughly 160 Thompson colours only twenty can be considered identical at this stage; the others do not compare favourably as most appear either lighter or darker than the original. This information (obtainable from Vitrum Signum, *see* Useful Addresses) is very valuable for enamellers who have some small amounts of Thompson enamels left and want to continue to select those particular hues or to choose an alternative enamel to substitute for an original Thompson colour if a piece of enamelled work over ten years old has to be repaired. Be aware of the problems of lead-based enamels when you are using them.

SARAH WILSON

Sarah uses delicate and subtle colouring in her recent pieces to create atmospheric enamels. A series of conical vases, about 100mm high, are based loosely on the seasons and the turning of the year. She describes the colours in her autumnal vase as muted shades of browns, greys and reds, while vestiges of distressed gold leaf give the effect of dying and wrinkled leaves. Her vase dedicated to the winter months has evocative icy violet greys, pale turquoises and silver flux, colours which swirl over the carved low relief imagery with long sharp streaks of silver foil suggesting shards of ice.

Variation in Batch Production

When enamels are supplied from the manufacturer there may be a variation between batches of the same colour. Do not assume that the new colour will match your previous one – always test before using it.

BELOW LEFT: Vases in engraved silver and champlevé (spring).

BELOW: Vases in engraved silver and champlevé (autumn and winter). 2001. Sarah Wilson.

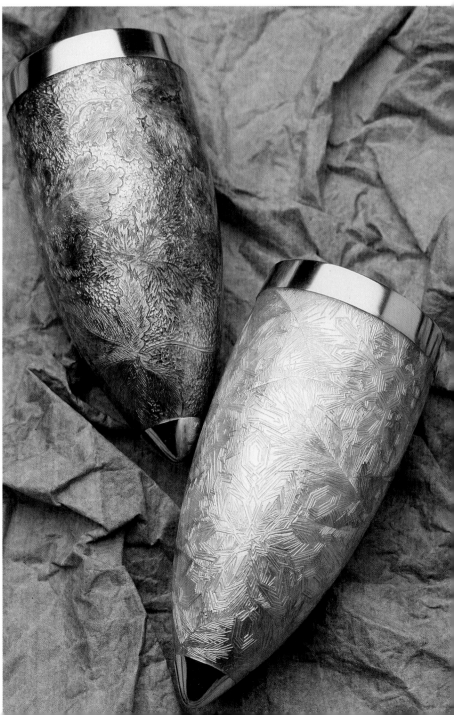

Sarah trained at Sir John Cass School of Art and subsequently became an indentured apprentice to Phil Barnes. She has recently returned to the college and teaches part time. Sarah has won nine awards in the last twelve years for her work in the Goldsmiths Craft Council Competitions and was made a Freeman of the Goldsmiths' Company in 1994. She has exhibited nationally and internationally with the British Society of Enamellers and has shown recently at the Fire and Ice Showcase Exhibition at Studio Fusion, London, and in Fusion at Bilston Craft Gallery, Wolverhampton.

Sarah's account of her takeover of the enamel outlet at Camden Mews from Gudde, the hectic removal of all the stock from Camden and the launch of Vitrum Signum is memorable, as are her invaluable notes on the trials of new enamels. She writes with humour, honesty and enthusiasm, and is a pillar of knowledge and advice in her role as supplier and mentor.

PREPARATION AND APPLICATION OF ENAMEL

Today many enamellers use ready-ground enamel colours, and certainly they are of much higher quality than ever before. A lot of time is saved by not having to grind the lump enamel, but it must be remembered that even the pre-ground enamels still need to be washed until any sign of silt or white cloudy water has been eliminated. Depending on the area in which the enameller lives and the quality of the tap water, it may be used for the first few washings but, however good it is, the final three or four washings should be in purified water and so should be any subsequent washings after acidulation. The water from an ordinary household water filter jug is a reasonable substitute for purified water.

Because of the need for the utmost clarity and perfection of colour, it is preferable to use lump enamel, particularly when

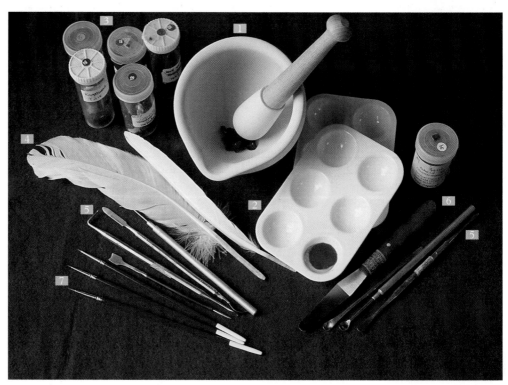

Enamelling equipment.

1 *Pestle and mortar*
2 *Dishes for keeping enamel in while in use*
3 *Containers of pre-ground enamel powder*
4 *Quills*
5 *Assortment of interesting enamelling tools*
6 *Palette knife*
7 *Fine sable paint brushes*

working in plique à jour. Enamel in lump form will keep its colour and capability when stored for a long time, whereas ready-prepared enamel will start to lose its colour, especially if left in the light. Grind the grains down to the size necessary for the type of enamelling being carried out and the colour being ground, and grind only sufficient for the purpose in hand. Enamellers in the fourteenth and fifteenth centuries are known to have ground their enamels as they needed them and to have resmelted them at the end of each day, because it was recognized how quickly ground enamels would decompose when in contact with water.

Grinding from the Lump

Place the lump of enamel in a piece of thick cloth or a very thick plastic bag and, with a few sharp blows with a hammer, reduce it

to manageable-sized pieces without losing any of the small fragments. A pestle and mortar is required for the next process, ideally one made of agate, but a fully vitrified, acid-proof porcelain one is generally an acceptable substitute. Put a small quantity of enamel lumps in the mortar, and fill it to about two-thirds capacity with water. Position the pestle over the enamel and give it one or two sharp taps with a wooden mallet to crush the lumps even smaller; sometimes it is possible just to press firmly against the lumps. Pour the water away and add enough fresh water to just cover the pieces.

Use a firm pressure and circular rocking motion with the pestle to start the grinding. As the process proceeds the milky white impurities or silt must be poured away from time to time and fresh water added. You can tap the handle of the pestle lightly on the side of the mortar to facilitate the separation of silt and enamel but take care to pour away only the silt. At the beginning of the grinding process you should apply a fair amount of pressure with the pestle, but should slowly reduce this as the final stages are reached to ensure perfect regularity of the grains. Continue washing and grinding until the enamel has the appearance appropriate to the colour or type of enamel being ground. This usually resembles fine sand but it is important not to grind some enamels to excess. Transparent and translucent colours, and particularly the reds, should be moderately coarse although regular, and excessive grinding will mar the brilliant limpidity after firing. However, opaque

Mesh Sizes	
mesh size	particle size
325	0.004mm
200	0.074mm
150	0.099mm
100	0.117mm
80	0.149mm

Grinding the enamel.

enamels, and especially the whites, are improved by fine grain grinding.

Acidulation

Acidulation is the process by which any minuscule parts of metal or free alkalis, which have been disengaged during the grinding process, are removed. It also eliminates any small particles of dust or organic matter that may have been present in the grinding water.

If acidulation is required (and this is not always the case), pour about eight to ten drops of pure nitric acid on to the damp enamel grains while still in the mortar. In the case of very soft enamels you will need only three to five drops. Stir the grains and the acid very gently with the pestle in a circular movement for three to five minutes; you must be gentle to avoid further grinding and the creation of fresh silt. The acid must be washed away immediately and totally removed by at least six washings. The nitric acid also has the effect of hardening the enamels and this is why they should not be left in the acid too long.

The enamel is now ready for use and should be stored in small, airtight, well-labelled jars with the enamel covered with pure water. The enamel should be kept covered at all times except when actually being used, as the normal atmosphere carries dust and small particles that will pollute it. Once the enamel has been prepared it can be stored in airtight jars for several days. However, on the day the enamels are used they should be thoroughly washed again to remove any white silt that may have accumulated. The importance of this washing process cannot be sufficiently stressed if muddy colours are to be avoided and pinholes, cracks and bubbles eliminated.

Pouring away the silt.

APPLICATION OF WET ENAMEL

Preparation and Tools

Ideally enamels should be laid in as soon as possible after preparation, in a workshop that is scrupulously clean and free of dust. It is not always possible to work in an ideal situation, but you should try to eliminate as much contamination as possible by scrubbing down the area to be worked in. Prepare the piece to be enamelled by washing and degreasing it with ammonia in hot soapy water. After this it is important not to touch it with even the cleanest hands, as the natural oil of the skin will contaminate the metal, so always use a pair of clean tweezers to handle the piece. If possible, place the article to be enamelled on a piece of flat board that can be revolved smoothly so that each part is easily reached.

There are a number of implements used by craftsmen to deposit the enamel on to the metal, each of which has been selected by the individual to suit personal working traits. These include the old-fashioned (but still used) quill, different-sized steel points, fine sewing needles held in small pin vices, tiny spoons (often hammered out of brass wire), old dental probes and fine water-colour brushes. Apart from the preferred tool, it is useful to have to hand some soft tissues or small clean pieces of soft cloth such as worn linen, and some blotting paper.

Laying in Enamel

The classic method of laying in the enamel is to pick up small amounts of the damp grain with the chosen implement and transfer it to the metal, where it is spread to the required thickness. By careful handling of the implement the enamel can be spread very evenly and pushed into all the corners of the cells. It is best to apply two or three successive thin layers, firing between each one, particularly with transparent enamels. As each layer is applied it is good practice to lay a piece of clean cloth or blotting paper over the wet enamel surface and gently press down on it using a small spatula. This is not only to remove any surplus water but also to pack the enamel down and to release any air bubbles. At this point the edge of the piece may also be given a few gentle taps with the spatula to help the enamel grains form an even layer. After this the enamel should be covered to prevent dust falling on to it and left to dry on the top of the kiln.

Larger surfaces, either flat or curved, can be coated in enamel with a larger brush if preferred, but it is advisable in this case to mix the enamel with gum tragacanth in filtered water. This will prevent the enamel from running. When gum is used it is vital that all the water is evaporated out of the enamel before it is fired or blisters will form, which can break away leaving patches of bare metal.

Sifting Dry Enamel

All sizes of work can be enamelled with a dry application by sprinkling the cleaned, ground and dried enamel through a fine sieve. The metal to receive the powder should be sprayed with a solution of gum tragacanth or similar before the sifting takes place. This method of applying the enamel

---

Troubleshooting

There are various reasons for pinpricks, small hollows, black spots and bubbles in the finished work:

- The enamel was not washed sufficiently
- The metal was not degreased
- Gum tragacanth was overused and applied too thickly
- Enamels were stored too long
- Air bubbles were created because the enamel was not pressed down or tapped
- Black spots result when a mix of soft and hard enamels are fired at high temperature

is used when stencilling or screen printing, or for scraffito, and a number of layers of different colours can be sifted, overlaid and fired to produce interesting patterns and colour variations.

Cleaning in Acid

When cleaning an enamel piece it can be put in a maximum solution of 10 per cent sulphuric acid, cold or warm, but it should not be left in the solution for any longer than is absolutely necessary to clean the metal. If the acid solution is too strong or the time period too long the acid will attack the enamel surface and create an indelible watermark or total porosity. In general, transparent enamels are acid resistant, but if opaque or opalescent enamels are being used they must be protected with a colourless resist such as lacquer or nail varnish. If leaded enamels and lead-free enamels are being used on the same piece it is inadvisable to place them in acid as the lead-free enamels are not acid-resistant.

COUNTER-ENAMELLING

The high temperatures required to fuse enamel to metal create a problem in that these materials expand and contract unequally when heated and cooled. This can lead to distortion of the piece and the cracking of part or all of the enamel. For this reason it is almost always necessary to apply an equal amount of enamel to the reverse of the piece, thus creating an enamel-metal-enamel sandwich that keeps the metal stable. This is called counter-enamelling.

Counter-enamelling is vital on thin gauges of precious metals, especially on large areas such as plaques, vases and bowls. It is advisable to counter-enamel using the same enamel or at least an equivalent enamel with the same firing temperature. The practice of using the silt enamel left over from washing and grinding is not recommended on precious metals,

although it is possible to use an appropriate flux, provided that the thickness of the flux corresponds to the number of layers on the front surface.

When thicker gauges of metal are used (16 gauge or greater), for example when the metal is to be engraved or chased, counter-enamelling is unnecessary. Many jewellers prefer to make their pieces in thicker gauges of metal to save having to counter-enamel, especially if the piece is complex. A silver alloy that does not need to be counter-enamelled even at 11 gauge is 1715 hardenable silver (*see* Chapter 3).

FIRING AND KILNS

The instructions below are general firing instructions that apply to all the techniques of enamelling; the relevant chapters later in the book deal with any specific variations. Transparent colours need to be fired high and fast to achieve clarity, while opaques and the second firing of opalescents need to be taken at a lower temperature. The metal determines how high the temperature can be and details of the metals can be found in Chapter 3.

• The enamel must be absolutely dry before being placed in the kiln.
• Too low a temperature may result in poor colours.
• When removing the piece from the kiln, put it in a warm place to cool slowly to avoid cracking.
• A piece can take days to make, hours to pack, seconds to fire and a moment's distraction to spoil. Concentration is vital.

Choosing a Kiln

Buying a kiln is a crucial step for an enameller. It is an expensive capital item and it pays to identify in some detail the operations for which it is intended – for example firing enamels, casting, sintering PMC, hardening 1715 silver and kiln soldering – and its type of construction. Making a mistake at this stage is likely to be very annoying and frustrating at some future date. Consider all the following points before buying:

- Efficiency: the kiln should reach working temperatures quickly and be capable of maintaining a constant heat.
- Optimum size: there is no point in buying a large kiln if all the work is miniature, but a small kiln may limit the scale of your future pieces so think ahead. Bear in mind that the larger the kiln, the more power it will need to reach the required temperature, so will be more expensive to run.
- Heat source: the kiln can be electricity- or gas-powered, and low-pressure gas can also be used.

Kiln Temperature Colours		
	°C	°F
Dull cherry red	700+	(1300+)
Cherry red	760+	(1400+)
Bright cherry red	800+	(1450+)
Orange red	850+	(1550+)
Orange yellow	900+	(1600+)
Yellow white	950+	(1650+)
(All figures are approximate.)		

- Safety features: flame failure devices and power trip switches should be given consideration.
- Construction: the kiln door should be easy to open and close one-handed. The size of the firing chamber and door should be in proportion to the intended work.

Kiln and kiln equipment.

1 *Kiln*
2 *Pyrometer*
3 *Large palette knife*
4 *Long-handled tongs*
5 *Steel mesh trivet*
6 *Kaowool ceramic fibre*
7 *Mica*

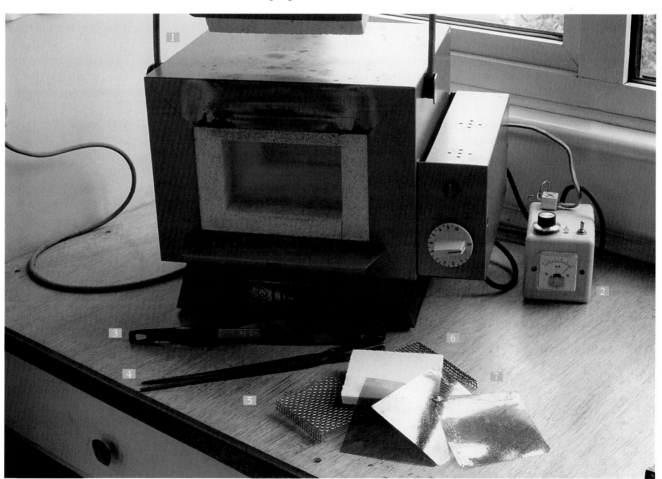

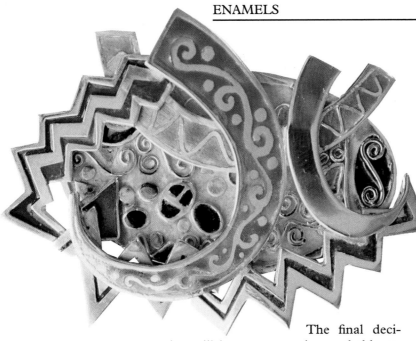

plugs into a 13 amp socket on the control unit and the control unit plugs into the mains electricity. The temperature range is 200–1000°C (392–1832°F) and the control is ±1°C over the temperature range.

There are two distinct designs of electric kiln. One is a muffle type, which has the heating elements wound round the exterior of a fireclay case and is then insulated with heat-resistant material before being enclosed in a steel case. The element type of kiln has the heating elements inserted inside the firing chamber and they are visible when the kiln door is open.

It is essential that all kilns are fitted with a safety device that isolates the electrical current from the elements when the door is open. The risk of an electric shock is obvious with the element type of kiln, but do not assume that if no element is visible there is no chance of receiving a shock. As enamel deposits erode the fireclay, the kiln floor starts to wear through and, although the element may not be visible, there is a possibility of a shock if tools are used that are not insulated. Many imported kilns do not have a safety device fitted.

The introduction of the gas-fired kiln for enamelling appears to have eliminated many of the problems of the electric kiln. The kiln achieves working temperatures quickly and 800°C (1472°F) can be reached in ten minutes. It appears to be easily maintained in the event of any problems.

The final decision will be a compromise, probably related to the kiln sizes available, although there are manufacturers who will build a kiln to individual specifications, if the additional expense is warranted. The reliability of the equipment is a high priority.

Regulating the temperature is vital to enamelling processes; therefore the quality and type of the pyrometer and the thermocouple are most important. The thermocouple senses the temperature inside the kiln and the pyrometer controls the heat to a set level and displays the temperature. There is a kiln control unit on the market that can be added to a kiln purchased without built-in controls. This has a temperature probe that fits into the kiln; the kiln

Kiln Temperature Effects on Enamels		
649–704°C (1200–1300°F)	Dark red	This will not fire enamels to a finished state but is the correct temperature for grisaille and china painting
760–816°C (1400–1500°F)	Cherry red	Produces an 'orange peel' effect, a preliminary firing
816–843°C (1500–1550°F)	Light cherry red	Fast high firing temperature for standard silver
843–871°C (1550–1600°F)	Cherry to orange	For final firing on gold, pure silver and 1715 alloy silver
871–899°C (1600–1650°F)	Orange yellow	Kiln soldering heat
(All figures are approximate.)		

3 PRECIOUS METALS FOR ENAMELLING

By applying identical enamels to various metals it is possible to build up a picture of how different colours come out on different metals. Here, fourteen samples of precious metals have been used as a ground for eight identical enamels, all fired at the same temperature to make direct comparison possible. The layout of the eight enamel examples, A–H (*see* below), is constant in all samples of enamel on metals. Blue flux was used under the enamels where stated.

A   Jade   Thompson 1067
B   Dark Blue   Schauer 5424 (ST44)
C   Garnet   Schauer 111 (ST15)
D   Windsor Purple   Schauer 6945 Violet ST21
E   Violet   Soyer 104 Light Purple
F   Mid Turquoise Turquoise Blue   Soyer 186 Mid Blue
G   Rich Ruby Red   Kujaku 105B
H   Ruby Red   Kujaku 105A

ON MICA

This shows the true colours, unaffected by metal. These would be the colours apparent in plique à jour.

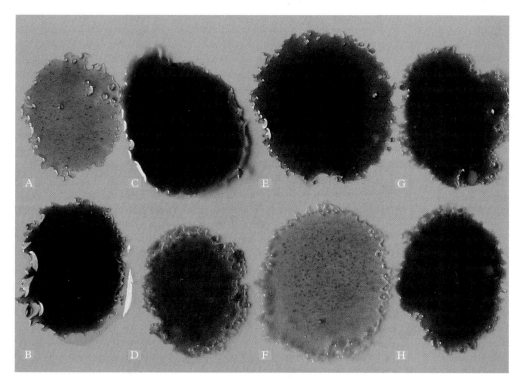

Enamel on mica.

Selection of 9K white gold, 18K yellow gold, coloured golds and platinum sheet, wire and tubing.

Silver sheet, wire and tubing.

1 2 3 *Silver wire*
4 *Reel of cloisonné wire*
5 *Silver sheet*
6 *Variety of silver tube*
7 *Ring tubing*
8 *Box tubing*
9 *Triangular tubing*
10 *Octagonal tubing*
11 *Silver hollow beads*

Pure Silver

SILVER

Pure Silver

Content: 99.9 per cent silver. Melting point: 960°C (1760°F)

The enamel colours on pure silver are generally very beautiful, with a few exceptions – for example, it is not good for reds, while some transparencies can fire with a yellow tinge. It is too soft to be used on its own unless it is at least 16 gauge, although, if there is a pure silver surround, it can be hardened by gentle tapping with a small hammer though great care has to be taken not to crack the enamel. Thinner sections of pure silver can be soldered to a base of standard silver or it can be used as a plaque and set in, or riveted to, standard silver. Because of its high melting point it can be fired at a higher temperature than standard silver.

	Without flux	With flux
A	true	good
B	true	good
C	good	slightly dark
D	true	good
E	orange	good
F	true	good
G	soft pink	true
H	true	true

Standard or Sterling Silver

Content: 92.5 per cent silver, 7.5 per cent copper. Melting point: 910°C (1670°F). Recommended firing temperature: 760–785°C (1400–1445°F)

Sterling silver is so called because up to 1920 all silver coinage in the United Kingdom was of this standard. It is the silver most used in the UK for enamelling. When enamelling large areas it is advisable to use a medium- to high-expansion rate enamel otherwise cracking may occur; this does not seem to apply to small areas. Because standard silver has a copper content the silver will oxidize, reducing the clarity and brilliant colour of transparent enamels when they are used directly on the silver. Use a first layer of silver flux to achieve clearer colours, or engrave immediately prior to enamelling to remove firestain and produce better colour.

	Without flux	With flux
A	good	good
B	good	good
C	too orange	good
D	good	good
E	too orange	good
F	good	good
G	too orange	good
H	too orange	good

Standard Silver

Enamel on pure silver.

Enamel on standard silver.

Hardenable Silver Alloy (1715)

Content: 99.65 per cent silver, 0.2 per cent magnesium, 0.15 per cent nickel. Melting point: 1000+°C (1840°F)

Hardenable silver is an alloy that was first produced by Johnson Matthey in the early 1970s. It has two qualities. The first is called N quality and is sold in an annealed state, being as soft and malleable as pure silver. This can be irreversibly hardened in a kiln. The second form is P quality, which is already in the hardened state. It can be used in a flat sheet and for pin wires and straight wires, but cannot be bent or manipulated as the metal will fracture. It is an excellent alloy for enamelling purposes because of its strength and because, lacking copper, it does not suffer from firestain. The working of this alloy is very different from any other metal and directions for its use should be followed exactly or problems may arise.

	Without flux	With flux
A	true	true
B	true	true
C	poor	true
D	good	true
E	poor	true
F	good	true
G	too orange	true
H	too orange	true

Florentine Finish
This is made with a liner engraver. It is a network of lines – parallel, cross-hatched or curved – that cover a surface with a texture. Different results can be obtained and experimenting will produce many interesting finishes to apply under transparent enamel.

Germanium Silver (Bright Sterling Silver)

Content: 92.5 per cent silver, 6.3 per cent copper, 1.2 per cent germanium. Melting point: 765–875°C (1410–1608°F)

This silver alloy has been developed by Thessco Ltd in conjunction with Peter Johns at Middlesex University, primarily as a firestain-resistant sterling silver. Thessco have said that when enamelling on this alloy the colours do not darken as expected on ordinary sterling silver and, at higher temperatures, the tarnish-resistance mechanism inhibits the wetting of the enamel. The results of personal tests were not encouraging.

Britannia Silver

Content: 96.3 per cent silver, 3.6 per cent copper. Melting point: 890–920°C (1635–1688°F)

RIGHT: Enamel on hardenable silver.

FAR RIGHT: Enamel on Britannia silver.

1715 Hardenable Silver

Britannia Silver

This alloy is often used for enamelling purposes. However, even though it only has half the copper content of standard silver it still has firestain and is quite soft to use for anything sizeable.

	Without flux	With flux
A	true	true
B	true	true
C	poor	good (pink)
D	good	very good
E	poor	true
F	good	good
G	poor	true
H	poor	true

Silver Precious Metal Clay and PMC Plus

Content: (after sintering) 99 per cent pure silver. Melting point: approximately 960°C (1760°F)

This new material is a mix of pure silver particles held in water and a non-toxic binder, and it has the feel of, and works in a similar way to, porcelain. After forming the clay it is kiln fired at 900°C (1652°F) and, once the water and binder have evaporated (a process called sintering) the article is left as pure silver, which can be enamelled, soldered and hallmarked. Precious Metal Clay needs up to two hours to sinter, depending on size and how much

shrinkage is acceptable. Precious Metal Clay Plus, which is a newer product, only takes ten minutes to sinter. A thermostatically controlled kiln is recommended (*see* Chapter 9).

	Without flux
A	true
B	true
C	poor
D	good
E	poor
F	true
G	good
H	good

Casting Silver

Content: pure silver with pure copper (standard silver)

When articles are cast they have a pure silver surface. If the enamelling is done without disturbing this pure silver layer the piece will remain fire free during the firing process. Better colour is often achieved if the area to be enamelled is subtly engraved or given a Florentine finish to give a bright finish through the enamel. However, cast objects are porous and problems may arise if the metal is not burnished to close the pores. It is preferable to cast in pure silver for enamelling. In the examples shown, all eight colours were used randomly.

Precious Metal Clay

Casting Silver

FAR LEFT: Enamel on PMC.

LEFT: Enamel on casting silver.

RIGHT: Enamel on pure gold.

FAR RIGHT: Enamel on 22K gold.

Pure 24K Gold

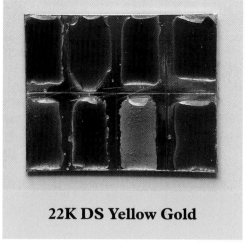

22K DS Yellow Gold

GOLD

Pure or Fine Gold

Content: 100 per cent gold. Melting point: 1063°C (1945°F)

The colour and purity of this metal allows the most brilliant colours to be produced; and, although it is too soft to be used on its own, it can be used as a decorative addition to a lesser karat gold. It can be soldered, set or riveted as an insert or as a plaque to a harder karat gold.

Without flux
A rich, almost true colour
B slightly green tone
C true
D not as vibrant as true colour
E slightly more red than true colour
F greener than true colour
G slightly more red
H slightly more red

Coloured Golds

There are many different coloured golds in the four main karats used in the UK. Other countries have even more, for example the USA has four shades of green, a blue and a purple. The golds described here are UK coloured golds that do not contain nickel or zinc in the alloy. They are from Cookson's stock and have been tested for use with enamels in a limited situation.

22K DS Yellow Gold
Content: 91.8 per cent gold, 3.18 per cent silver, copper. Melting point: approximately 1000°C/1700°F

This is a good metal for enamelling, too soft for use on its own but good for inlays. Because of the intense yellow colour the enamel blues often fire slightly green.

Without flux
A slightly green
B slightly green
C slightly orange
D good
E good, slightly pink
F greener than true
G good
H very slightly orange

18K HB Yellow Gold
Content: 75.0 per cent gold, 15.97 per cent silver, copper. Melting point: 905–960°C (1660–1760°F)

This is a very good metal to work and enamel. The colours are usually very true and often beautifully rich.

Without flux
A true
B good
C slightly orange
D good

18K Yellow Gold

Without flux
A   true
B   true
C   very good
D   true
E   orange
F   slightly green
G   true
H   true

Enamel on HB 18K yellow gold.

E   good
F   too green
G   good
H   good

18K GR Green Gold
Content: 75.1 per cent gold, 24.97 per cent silver. Melting point: 960–1170°C (1760–2138°F)

This very soft metal gives excellent colour for inlays. Most enamel colours work well and the metal can make an interesting contrast with other golds.

18K SW White Gold
Content: 75.1 per cent gold, 7.9 per cent silver, 17.0 per cent palladium. Melting point: 1300–1315°C (2372–2400°F)

This good high-karat gold is malleable and excellent to use in both sheet and wire. If polished before enamelling it will retain its lustre after firing. It gives precise enamel colours, especially the reds and pinks.

Without flux
A   true
B   true
C   a bit orange
D   good
E   true
F   true
G   true
H   true

18K GR Green Gold

18K SW White Gold

FAR LEFT: Enamel on 18K green gold.

LEFT: Enamel on SW 18K white gold.

RIGHT: Enamel on 18K MW white gold.

FAR RIGHT: Enamel on 9K white gold.

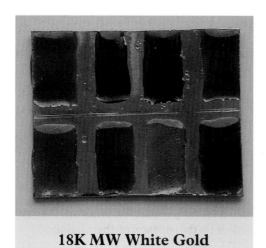

18K MW White Gold

9K White Gold

18K MW White Gold
Content: 75.1 per cent gold, 11.85 per cent silver, 13.0 per cent palladium. Melting point: 1180–1235°C (2156–2258°F)

Similar to SW white gold. This is a good metal for working and enamelling, but the metal looks dark and heavy when polished.

Without flux
A true
B true
C too orange
D true
E good, a bit pink
F good
G true
H true

9K White Gold
Content: 37.6 per cent gold, 54.6 per cent silver, copper. Melting point: 915–950°C (1680–1742°F)

A good low-karat gold for many blue and green enamels. Flux is needed under red enamels.

Without flux
A true
B true
C too orange
D true

E poor
F true
G too orange
H too orange

PMC Gold
Content: 100 per cent pure gold. Melting point: 1063°C (1846°F)

This new material is a mix of pure gold particles held in suspension in water with a non-toxic binder. It has the feel of, and works in a similar way to, porcelain although it is darker in colour. After forming the clay it is kiln fired at 1000°C (1832°F) and when the water and binder have evaporated, a process called sintering, the article is left as pure gold, which can be enamelled, soldered and hallmarked. PMC needs two hours to sinter. It is an expensive material so it may be advisable to gain experience first with silver PMC, which has the same properties. A thermostatically controlled kiln is recommended. No personal enamel tests have been made on this material.

PLATINUM

Content: 100 per cent platinum. Melting point: 1769°C (3217°F)

Platinum is a very beautiful metal with special characteristics, many of them

Platinum

Enamel on platinum.

Annealing and Soldering Platinum

Because of the high melting point of the harder platinum solders an ordinary gas torch gives insufficient heat to solder and a microweld is needed. A torch using oxygen and one of the fuel gases such as acetylene is needed to anneal. **Always wear protective darkened glasses when using an oxyacetylene torch or a microweld.**

---

unique, which make it quite different to work with from gold and silver. The different techniques you need to use this metal may at first seem a disadvantage, but in time you will find you have not only acquired useful techniques but also discovered new possibilities in making and decorating jewellery. Personal experience has shown that the lowest-melting platinum solder can be used with a gas/mouth blowtorch, as long as an enclosed area of firebrick is constructed to concentrate the heat and the firebrick is heated before the soldering starts.

Without flux

A true
B true
C true
D true
E true
F true
G true
H true

A drawback to using platinum is its high price, although it can be used in thinner gauges because of its extra weight and strength. There are other aspects that also have to be considered. It is easy to contaminate this metal and contamination is irreversible, so each time a piece of platinum is touched by any other metal, it must be cleaned in warm dilute hydrochloric acid (*see* Chapter 10). This cleaning must be done before any heat is applied otherwise any dust or particles of other metals will sink into the surface of the platinum and can then be removed only by refining or by cutting out the area and patching. Equally, only clean or new refractory blocks must be used during soldering and annealing – no other type of soldering blocks will do.

There is some doubt as to whether platinum can be enamelled at all and certainly the glass does not fuse with the platinum as the melting temperature of the metal is too high; this is why it is used as a backing for plique à jour enamel. However, as long as there is a surface for the enamel to key into, the cloisonné wires are slightly undercut and the cloison spaces small, there seems to be very little problem in holding in the enamel. There are several ways of treating the surface to be enamelled in order to key in the enamel: engine turning, engraving and roller printing will all give the enamel a good purchase.

The Micro Weld Flame Generator

This gives an intensely hot, clean, needle-point flame with an approximate temperature of 1850°C/3362°F capable of welding platinum and high-karat gold without the use of flux or solder. The gas produced is made from distilled water by electrolysis and is a mix of hydrogen and oxygen in the ratio of 2:1. Details are available from H.S. Walsh and Sons Ltd or Exchange Findings. (*See* Useful Addresses.)

Brooch in platinum, pure gold and cloisonné. 1996. Jeanne Werge-Hartley.

Working with Platinum

Platinum is a very easy metal to work as it is highly ductable and malleable, and drawing down fine wire for cloisonné is easy as long as dry soap powder is used as a lubricant.

The metalwork hardens more quickly than silver or gold and must be annealed more frequently. Annealing platinum is a two-stage process: the first stage is to relieve the stresses and the second stage to soften the metal. A large, bushy, blue oxidizing flame is needed, so a dispersion tip should be used of a size suitable for the amount of metal to be annealed. Stress is relieved at the same temperature at which silver is annealed and the colour of the metal is the same cherry red. It is best to stress relieve for a few minutes before proceeding to the annealing temperature of 983°C (1800°F), when the platinum glows bright orange, and you should maintain this temperature for at least thirty seconds to ensure correct annealing; obviously the length of time is determined by the size of the piece. The metal may then be air cooled or quenched in water.

Soldering is done the same way as with any precious metal except that flux is not necessary for any platinum solders under 1300°C (2372°F) since platinum does not oxidize. A liquid flux such as Auflux or FM solution can be useful to hold solder in place during heating, but use it sparingly and allow to dry before applying the heat. Like gold solder, platinum solder will not fill gaps, so all joints must be a perfect fit. In some cases gold solder can be used but usually only when joining gold to platinum. Because of the lack of oxidization there is virtually no polishing to be done when the piece is completed, provided all the components were well polished prior to assembly, soldering and enamelling.

Although the processes are complex and possibly time-consuming, the resulting enamel colours are well worth the extra work. If you fire the piece only once, the risk of the enamel not adhering is minimized.

Because of its malleability it is possible to beat platinum into leaf or foil to be applied under enamel as decoration in a similar way to gold foil.

SILVER SOLDERING TECHNIQUES PRIOR TO ENAMELLING

In general terms, when soldering a piece of work before enamelling, either to attach the fine wires for cloisonné techniques or to construct a complex piece, it is advisable to use the very hard enamelling solder often referred to as I.1 as much as possible and certainly on the areas that will eventually come into contact with the enamel. Hard and, if necessary, medium solder may be used on other joins as long as these are supported in the kiln by either mesh or heat-resistant paste to prevent the collapse of these parts. For example, the findings on the back of brooches, pendants, earrings and cufflinks can all be supported and covered in heat-resistant paste, but care must be taken to ensure that the paste does not come into contact with the enamel at any time. Enamelling solder can on occasions be difficult to flow and, if too

much heat is applied, pit holes in the metal may appear or the solder may be left as a lump that then has to be removed with a scraper. There are a number of ways that these problems can be overcome and the following suggestions may be of use.

It always helps to preheat the soldering block. Soldering blocks can be arranged to form a small enclosed area that will retain the heat, so that the heat that is applied to the metal is not absorbed by the blocks and the metal quickly achieves the temperature needed to get the solder to flow. It should go without saying that the metal must be clean and grease-free. An application of a flux, such as borax or FM solution, will keep the air from producing a layer of firescale, and using Auflux on the solder and joint will allow it to flow at a lower temperature.

The flux that can be of real value here is FM solution. This not only does the job of

---

FM Solution Recipe

It is essential to be accurate in measuring these ingredients.

Boric acid	53.2g
Sodium acid phosphate	35.0g
Sodium hydroxide	3.4g
Borax (powder)	35.0g
Distilled water	0.75l
Teepol	14.2ml

Mix all the chemicals together with the Teepol and the distilled water in a litre container and shake gently until dissolved. The distilled water can be added lukewarm to assist the mix.

Preventing Firestain
The metal must not be highly polished; the surface should be slightly matted with fine Garriflex or fine emery paper. Paint or spray the surface with the solution and allow to dry for maximum effect. The solution should always be clean so, to ensure this, it is best to work with small amounts and replace it frequently.

---

keeping the metal clean and the solder flowing easily but also does not bubble up and dirty the metal like borax does. If the solution is applied correctly the soldered piece should only require putting in water to clean it. Flattening the solder in the rolling mill, or hammering it to about 2 gauge, and cutting small paillons to go as close as possible to the seam helps you to solder neatly. In cloisonné one small rectangular strip of solder at either end of the wire should flow along under the wire, soldering the entire length to the metal base. If you place the piece on a wire mesh and heat from underneath, you will also speed up the flow.

There are several ways of inhibiting the solder from spreading on to other areas. Possibly the best known method is to use a little rouge powder in alcohol and apply with a small paintbrush, but this is not only messy but sometimes difficult to remove after heating. A simpler method is to draw on the metal with a soft pencil, or typewriter

Precious Metal Gauge Sizes (BMG)	
Gauge 2	0.241mm
Gauge 4	0.305mm
Gauge 6	0.406mm
Gauge 8	0.546mm
Gauge 10	0.711mm
Gauge 11	0.813mm
Gauge 12	0.889mm
Gauge 14	1.092mm
Gauge 16	1.295mm
Gauge 20	1.651mm
Gauge 24	2.083mm

correction fluid, but care should be taken with the latter as the fumes are thought to be dangerous when hot. At a Goldsmiths' Company research session some years ago, solder inhibitors were investigated and colloidal graphite proved to be excellent. This product is a commercial mix of graphite in alcohol and was used by the motor industry at that time.

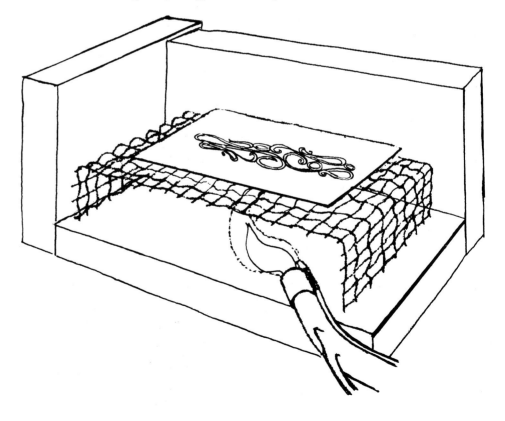

Soldering: directing heat under the wires.

If, after taking all these precautions, solder is still evident it must be removed before enamelling can begin, as otherwise it will cause the enamel to ping out and discolour any transparent enamels. The solder can be removed by careful use of a graver or scraper, or by using mounted grinding points on a flexi-drill, but this has to be done with care so that the actual surface of the metal is not damaged. Using Water of Ayr stone, sharpened to the shape which will fit, is possibly the safest method, if somewhat tedious. There is also another series of abrasive sticks on the market, consisting of compressed fibreglass, which can be used wet or dry and filed to any shape.

POLISHING METALS

Polishing precious metal is an art form in its own right and it is not surprising that in the trade there are specialist polishers who do nothing else but perfect their craft. For the artist enameller, who designs and makes one-off pieces or small batch productions, polishing is part of the whole process, and quite often the way a piece is finished and polished makes it very individual and personal to the maker. No matter how well a piece of silversmithing or jewellery is made and enamelled, the final effect can be spoilt by poor polishing – edges may be worn away and the surface lustre broken up by small scratch marks or residual firestain.

Many artist enamellers have been through a recognized jewellery or silversmithing course and are aware of the numerous methods of achieving a good finish to the metal surrounds of the enamelled areas. Some craftsmen tend to leave all the polishing processes until after the piece is finally soldered and enamelled, which often results in the finished piece not being as satisfactory as it really merits. To achieve the best results it is important for each part to be hand polished and

Polishing materials.

1. *Emery paper*
2. *Micron graded abrasive finishing sheets*
3. *Compressed glassfibre sticks*
4. *Cotton buds*
5. *Selection of flexi-drive mops and abrasive points*
6. *Fraizers or burrs*
7. *Glassfibre brush*
8. *Washing-out brush*
9. *Agate burnisher*
10. *Two polished steel burnishers*
11. *Diagrit*
12. *Scotchbrite*
13. *Garriflex*
14. *Selection of Water of Ayr stones and carborundum sticks*

protected against firestain and firescale before soldering to the next part. The soldering should be carried out on the back of the piece whenever possible. If this is done correctly, using an inhibitor to stop the solder flowing too far, there will be less likelihood of having to remove excess solder from the surface of the piece.

Preparation and Hand Polishing

Preparation of the metal starts with the use of graded emery papers. A coarse-grade No 2 can be used to remove all deep scratches and file marks, if there are any, as even these are preventable with a correct method of filing. Once these are removed a gradual succession of using finer grades can be used. Each time you change grades, cross grain, that is emery at 90 degrees to the previous marks and make sure that all the emery marks from the previous grade are removed before using the next finer grade. After using the final, pale green grade of the micron graded abrasive sheets, the metal is usually ready for enamelling or limited machine polishing or texturing to create a matt finish.

All British emery papers can also be bought as ready-made emery sticks; these can also be simply made by gluing strips of emery paper to lengths of wood approximately 30cm long by 3.5mm wide and

0.5mm deep. You can use the same method to cover other wooden shapes, for example a dowel – for polishing the inside of rings – and half round sections. Emery sticks are easier to use than paper on flat and shallow curved surfaces and a firmer pressure can be applied. They can also be covered with felt and chamois leather saturated with a polishing compound such as rouge powder. There are a number of useful polishing compounds available to allow access to intricate and awkward areas. Friction sticks made from compressed glassfibre can be shaped and reshaped by filing or sanding to whatever shape is required. Flexi-drive points of similar material can also be useful, but care should be taken not to create grooves or marks in the metal. Water of Ayr stone is another useful tool for working round difficult areas and removing scratches, and can also be shaped by filing. Abrasive flexible polishing blocks come in three grades – coarse, medium and fine – and can be safely used over enamel to remove any firestain or firescale from the metal.

Thrumming is a method of polishing narrow openings and other difficult areas, and involves using a length of polishing thread tied securely to the bench and covered in rouge powder paste. Pass the thread through the spaces that need attention and rub the piece up and down, watching that the threads do not make a groove in the metal. Rouge powder paste can also be used on cotton buds to reach difficult places.

Machine Polishing

The polishing machine should be avoided as long as possible by hand polishing to a stage where only a minimum polish is necessary on the machine. There are a number of different polishing mops and brushes that can be used on the machine and on a flexi-drive, plus a variety of polishing compounds, each serving a particular function.

Abrasive Papers

The grades of emery paper are 3, 2, 1, 0, 1/0, 2/0, 3/0 and 4/0 plus crocus or rouge papers. These grades also exist as silicon carbide (wet and dry) papers. Very fine American micron graded abrasive finishing sheets are highly recommended and can be bought by mail order from Rio Grande and other outlets in the USA. They come in six very fine grades and are easy to recognize as they are all different colours, made of extremely thin but very strong paper, and can be used wet or dry.

Polishing the metal around the enamel must be done with care and attention. If the metal has been hand polished correctly it may be sufficient to limit the mops to a calico one and bristle brushes of varying sizes suited to the scale of the piece. Charge the mop with either Tripoli or Hyfin (a white polish used usually on steel but experience has shown it to be good for silver as well). Hold the piece firmly against the bottom quarter of the revolving mop, turning it often to avoid wearing away the edges (*see* Chapter 10). It is possible to get new scratches from the grit in the compound if the metal is held incorrectly and the mop is allowed to 'tickle' the surface.

In order to prevent the compound contaminating the next mop, wash the piece thoroughly in hot soapy water containing a few drops of ammonia. Apply a small amount of rouge compound to the soft swansdown mop and again push the metal up into the mop and turn it often to prevent wearing down the crisp edges. Once a good lustre has been achieved, wash it again in hot soapy water and ammonia, then rinse in clean hot water and place in clean sawdust to dry. If the piece has intricate detail, an ultrasonic cleaner can be very helpful and, as long as the liquid is only a hot soapy solution with a few drops of ammonia, it does not harm the enamel in any way.

Necklace in hardenable silver, 18K gold and cloisonné. 1992. Jeanne Werge-Hartley.

Finishes

Different kinds of surface can be arrived at using a variety of tools, such as a fibreglass brush, soap scouring pads, Scotch Brite with a slurry of pumice powder (240 mesh) or an assortment of dentist-type drills used in a flexi-drive. Swirling patterns or cross-hatching can be achieved by using a sharp point, while sand blasting (protect the enamel very carefully as the blast can rip off poor quality tapes) creates an interesting texture. You can arrive at many other effects through experimentation. Remember that textured surfaces often look more interesting if they are contrasted with a well-polished area.

OXIDATION HARDENING SILVER (1715 HARDENABLE SILVER ALLOY)

In 1971 the Worshipful Company of Goldsmiths introduced a new silver alloy, called hardenable silver, which was manufactured

Brooches in hardenable silver, 18K gold, cloisonné and basse taille. 1996. Jeanne Werge-Hartley.

by Johnson Matthey Metals under the code name 1715. A number of practising jewellers were invited by Peter Gainsbury to take part in a week-long seminar in London funded by the Technical Advisory Committee to investigate a number of new products and ideas. Amongst these was the opportunity to work with and discover the potential of the new alloy.

1715 silver is a very soft and malleable metal in its annealed state (N quality). The important attribute of this metal is that it can be irreversibly hardened by heating it in a kiln for two hours at 800°C (1472°F). The oxygen circulating in the kiln reacts with the magnesium and the nickel in the metal to create the hardened state (P quality).

The implications for its use in enamelling are obvious, the main one being the absence of copper (therefore no firestain), which allows the majority of enamels to fire at a near perfect colour. The strength of the hardened silver also enables pieces to be made in thinner sections of sheet without having to counter-enamel, and three-dimensional pieces are easier to construct.

Advance planning is important when using this metal. The design and construction of a piece has to be thought out quite carefully, as any shaping, such as doming, bending of wires or curving of the metal, must be done prior to hardening. Once it is in its hardened state it is difficult to change the shape without causing stresses in the metal, which can eventually lead to cracks and faults in the enamels. Polishing the metal in its annealed state is good practice, as once the silver is hardened it is more difficult to eliminate any scratches, but any grease must be carefully removed before hardening as this would inhibit the hardening process. The silver will retain its lustre because of the lack of firestain and will often need only a final rouge polish.

Annealing

With N quality silver it is often unnecessary to anneal during the construction of the piece. For example, a length of 3.2mm diameter wire can be drawn to 0.6mm diameter without annealing, and it can then be worked further and rolled to

Brooch in hardenable silver and enamel with an integral fastening. 1986. Sarah Macrae.

NOTE: Cookson have made the decision to delete this excellent alloy from their stock.

Rings in hardenable silver, 18K yellow gold and cloisonné. 2000. Jeanne Werge-Hartley.

Brooches in hardenable and standard silver with gold wires and foils and niello. 2000. Sheila McDonald.

0.2mm ribbon or cloisonné wire. Although large amounts of this alloy should be annealed in a salt bath, small amounts are quite easily softened, if necessary, by heating with a blowtorch for a few minutes at 300–350°C (572–662°F). To make sure you do not overheat the metal, mark the surface with soap. When it begins to char, the metal should be quenched at once to prevent the piece from case hardening. A coating of flux will help to stop air reaching the metal and minimize the chance of surface hardening.

Soldering

All soldering must be done after the hardening process as the solder joints would weaken after two hours in the kiln. Because the silver is now so strong the solder joints become the weakest point, which is the reverse of soldering standard silver. Butt joints are not strong enough and therefore you should construct joints that increase the metal-to-metal contact, such as tapered overlaps (scarphs). One way to achieve a strong joint is to flow solder on the two separate parts to be joined, using an inhibitor to prevent the solder from showing on the front of the piece. File away any excess solder and, using binding wire to hold the two pieces together, heat rapidly to flow the solder to give a good strong join.

Each time the silver is heated a white layer of magnesium appears on the surface, which must be removed before attempting to solder, because otherwise the solder would only attach to the magnesium layer and would peel off. The magnesium layer is easily removed with either a piece of fine Garriflex abrasive or fine emery paper. Enamelling solder flows easily using Auflux or FM flux. There is no need to flux the silver, except possibly the area being joined, to assist the solder to flow. The silver does not melt until over 1000°C (1832°F) and, to allow the solder to flow before the magnesium deposit reappears, it is best to heat the whole piece as quickly as possible. It is not necessary to use 1715 cloisonné wire – pure silver is acceptable as the base is so rigid.

Hardening

The hardening process must be done correctly, at the exact temperature and for the appropriate period of time. The hardening time is two hours per millimetre thickness. The metal starts to harden from the outside and if it is not completely hardened the centre core will be weak and crystalline, which will give structural problems. Provided that the kiln is at the right temperature – 800°C (1472°F) – it is impossible to cause any adverse effects by leaving the piece in the kiln for too long, so if the kiln time is difficult to calculate, add on a sufficient margin to be certain of hardening. The presence of oxygen in the kiln is vital to the process, so air must be allowed into the kiln via the peep hole or by keeping the door fractionally open. The air must be able to circulate round each piece, which should be placed on a mesh and not allowed to overlap.

Enamelling

Before starting to enamel, all traces of the magnesium film must be removed, because, as in soldering, the enamel may peel off the magnesium layer and in any case the magnesium does not allow the true enamel colour to appear. Fine emery or Garriflex abrasive will remove the layer, or the surface may be scratched or engraved to create a pattern beneath the enamel. When using 1715 for plique à jour, where the contact is minimal, the removal of the magnesium film is doubly important. Enamels will fire to their true colour over this alloy although most of the reds still need a flux beneath them; it is a sensible idea to test fire the enamels to be used.

Polishing

If you hand polish before starting to put the pieces together the final polishing required should be minimal. Continue to hand polish as much as possible and if a final machine lustre is required, do not apply much pressure or allow the surface to get hot, as this can produce a thin bloom that obscures a mirror finish.

*The Millennium
Bridge Water Vessel
2000. The Royal
Collection © 2001,
Her Majesty Queen
Elizabeth II.
Jane Short.*

4 CHAMPLEVE

HISTORY

The name champlevé derives from the French words 'champs', meaning field, and 'levé', meaning lifted or raised, and describes a technique where recesses (the 'fields') are cut out of the metal to receive the enamel. When packed and fired the enamel can be said to be 'raised', flush with the surrounding metal. This method possibly achieves the strongest combination of metal and enamel of all enamelling techniques and is suitable for larger areas, both flat and shaped.

Champlevé was the first method to be developed of producing a decorative surface of colour on metal, and the oldest remaining examples are from the Mycenaean culture from 1400 BC. The depressions would have been hammered into the gold artefacts, and blue glass then fused into these areas. Some earlier examples of Egyptian jewellery give the illusion of enamel work, but this was actually accomplished by gluing shaped glass pieces into strips of metal framing. The Celts used champlevé technique, both casting the metal and cutting the recesses with tools,

Potpourri dish in silver and champlevé. Phil Barnes.

Potpourri dish (detail).
Phil Barnes.

and their enamelling was well established before the Romans came to north-west Europe. These early examples were basically cast or chiselled in bronze and the colour that predominated was opaque red.

Almost identical techniques were used in Romano-British pieces, but the opaque colour range was extended to include blue, white, and green as well as red. There seems to be little champlevé enamelling of importance after this period until the twelfth century, when the influence of the complex and figurative Byzantine cloisonné enamels reached the goldsmiths' workshops in western Europe. Here, although the beautiful colours and naturalistic designs of the Byzantine cloisonné

were adopted, the method used continued to be champlevé.

Limoges in France became the most important centre for champlevé and continued to be so well into the fourteenth century, but after this the naturalistic style almost disappeared except for heraldic purposes, where it has persisted to the present day. Whereas in the main brass and copper were used in champlevé pieces, precious metals form the background for nearly all heraldic work and ceremonial insignia. Opaque enamel is usually preferred for champlevé but transparents can and are used, and can look very beautiful if foils are incorporated or a surface finish is made with the graver.

Sculptural form (22cm) in silver and champlevé. Jane Short.

City of Portsmouth University Mace (detail) in silver and 18K gold (enamelled by Phil Barnes). 1993. Jeanne Werge-Hartley.

CHAMPLEVE TECHNIQUES

The walls of the cells that will contain the enamel are made by carving, engraving or etching away the metal to leave the required wall thickness. Varying the widths and regularity of the lines introduces a liveliness and innovative quality to the design. Occasionally the walls are so delicate it becomes difficult to distinguish the difference between champlevé and cloisonné work.

There are three main methods of manufacturing the cells that hold the enamel – appliqué, engraving and etching – and several variations and ideas that can be developed from these three methods depending on the dexterity and imagination of the designer enameller.

Appliqué Method

Possibly the easiest method to start with, and also the one that presents most possibilities for innovation, is sometimes referred to as the appliqué technique. This is

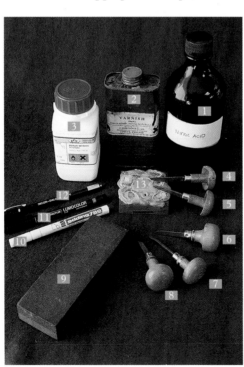

Engraving and etching equipment.

1. *Nitric acid*
2. *Rhinds stop-out*
3. *Ferric nitrate*
4. 5. 6. 7. 8.
   Scorpers and spitzsticks
9. *Sharpening oil stones*
10. *Edding paint marker*
11. *Permanent marker*
12. *Decon Dahler pen*
13. *Setters cement on wood*

because the cells are saw pierced out of sheet metal, which is then soldered onto a base piece of metal. The top piece is generally cut from standard silver at about 8 gauge while the base needs to be thicker and pure silver at around 12 gauge, depending on the scale of the whole piece. Variations to these measurements depend on the individual maker and the type of metal used. On small pieces pure silver could be used for both layers.

Once you have decided on the design for the saw piercing, transfer it to the metal by drawing freehand or tracing it onto the metal after covering the metal with a fine film of plasticine. To saw out

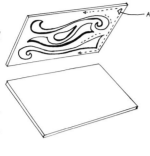

Place solder under top saw-pierced sheet and flow round the edges. Flux and bind together, heat from underneath until solder appears as a line round the outside edge.

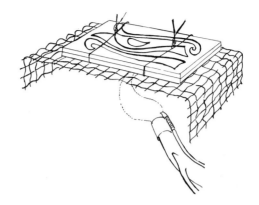

The appliqué method.

the cells, drill a hole close to the inner edge of the scribed line to conserve as much of the centre as possible. Pass the saw blade through and tighten it in the frame. A gentle sawing action while moving both the angle of the saw and the metal should give a clean shape, while a lubricant such as soap or beeswax helps the saw blade to cut through the metal smoothly. The shapes should be kept simple and without sharp corners, which can cause fractures or cracks in the enamel. When you have finished sawing you must neaten the edges of the cell walls with a half-round needle file before the pieces are soldered together. The base plate should be sawn out slightly larger than the top piece so there is a very slight lip when the pieces are put together. Clean the saw-pierced layer, coat it with flux and place it on a wire mesh underside up, then apply small paillons of enamelling solder to the underside. This way the hot flame can be directed underneath to allow the solder to flow across the surface. If there is an uneven layer of solder file away the excess, leaving a thin covering, before fluxing again and securing the two pieces together with either binding wire or cotter pins ready for soldering.

One of the things that can cause the enamel to discolour and crack is the presence of solder. To prevent the solder from flowing into the cells while the two pieces are joined, use a solder inhibitor inside the cells before heating. A quick way to do this, which is easy to clean away afterwards, is to use a soft B pencil to draw a thick line round the inside of the cell. Apart from using mesh to support the work while soldering, which allows the heat to get all round the work, it helps to build a three-sided enclosed area with fire bricks so the heat is not dissipated and can be controlled more easily.

Once the solder can be seen as a thin silver line around the outside edge and the piece is together, cool it, remove the binding wire or cotter pins and give the piece a good scrub with pumice slurry to remove the inhibitor. If findings such as brooch or earring fastenings are needed they should be soldered on at this point, but remember

Standard silver coated and heated with and without FM flux solution

Standard silver sheet heated, half protected by FM solution, and the other half showing the firestain.

Acids and Firestain

It should be stressed that sulphuric acid will only remove light firescale (CuO), not deeper firestain (CuO_2). Only repeated dips in pure nitric acid will do this, which can be unpleasant and dangerous. It is far better to prevent it from forming in the first place.

to protect the front from firestain. Medium solder can be used on the back of a piece as long as the findings are covered in Diewersol Cool Paste while the enamelling process takes place.

If the standard silver has been coated correctly with FM flux, there should be very little if any firestain to remove, and cleaning in dilute sulphuric acid, alum or safety pickle will remove any firescale (CuO) and any residue left from the flux. If small areas do appear they can be removed by rubbing over with Garriflex abrasive or gently scraping away with a sharp three-cornered scraper. In a more complex item small sticks of compressed glassfibre, which can be shaped to fit into odd corners, and Water of Ayr stones are invaluable.

If the solder has flowed correctly, once the two parts are finally polished they should appear as one solid sheet. It is practical to leave the filing and polishing of the edge until the enamel has been fired, but both the front and reverse surfaces should be cleaned, scratches eliminated and semipolished. The more that can be done at this stage, the less has to be done when the enamelling is complete, so the chance of damaging the enamel is minimized. The enamel is applied in the same way as for any other method (*see* Chapter 2).

Variations
The above process is a simple introduction to the champlevé technique, and it is easy to build on. Although this method is primarily thought of as one for opaque enamels,

transparents can be used and can look very attractive over texture. A textured surface can be created with an engraving tool or decorative punches, or you can make impressions on the base before soldering the two parts together by imprinting cut-paper, textured-paper or fabric patterns through a rolling mill. Gold and silver foil shapes can be held at the bottom of the cells with gum until the enamel is laid on top, using the foil either flat or scrunched slightly to give different reflective surfaces. The foil can also be given a specific pattern if great care is taken. Instead of engraving a pattern on the metal to show through the enamel, you could also use decorative punches to produce an interesting surface. Colours should be kept to the pale tints as far as possible because dark colours allow less light through and may appear black. If a dark colour is necessary it can be made shallower and brought to the same depth as the other colours with layers of flux, allowing the colour to shine through.

Using fine square 18K or pure gold wire to edge the cells gives a special effect. If the wire is the same height as the cell and made to fit very tightly, it can be kept in place with a small amount of gum tragacanth until the enamel is fired. Altering the shape of the wire, for example introducing scallops and zigzags, could change even the most simple piece into quite a different design.

Engraving and Carving

This is a very brief introduction to the methods involved in this exacting and specialized technique. To be a competent engraver takes skill and practice, and for a master craftsman a professional training is essential. For the purposes of this book, it is hoped that a small amount of information will encourage an interest sufficient to pursue the subject by reading specialist books and seeking tuition from a competent instructor. The aim here is to give sufficient information to allow you to attempt simple engraving for champlevé enamelling

Basic Tool List

- Metal scriber or sturdy metal point in a handle
- Scorpers for outlining
- Flats of varying sizes for removing the flat areas or 'fields'
- Spitzsticks for corners and trueing up edges
- Handles, half-mushroom shape
- Setter's cement or shellac to hold work securely on a block of wood
- Sharpening oilstone, available in coarse and medium grit
- Oil
- Methylated spirit for cleaning
- Tweezers
- Flat file, burnisher
- Sandbag, five or six inches (150mm or 200mm)

purposes. You could start by practising on a piece of aluminium. Apart from the actual skills needed to handle the scorpers and engraving tools, knowing how to take care of them and keep them sharp is important, and very necessary to achieve any progress or success. As confidence grows and you find you need to carry out more complex shapes, you will discover there are many sizes of engraver to work with, and that everybody has his or her own particular favourite, particularly for basse taille work.

It is important to ensure that the graver is the right length to hold. When fixed into its handle it should reach from the cup of the palm to the top knuckle of the forefinger or the top of the thumb. Gravers need to be kept very sharp and consequently great care must be taken when using these tools, and the point must be protected when not in use. Stick it in a wine bottle cork.

Sharpening the Tools
Gravers have to be ground to the correct angle on a grinding stone. To keep the gravers in a good working condition they should be sharpened on an oilstone or carborundum stone with a little oil such as Three in One. Using a steady pressure and making sure that the tool is held at a 45-degree angle, move it up and down the stone. The graver must not be allowed to rock as this will round the edge of the face. A slight burr will appear at the edge of the flat face, which can be removed by jabbing the tip of the graver into a block of wood or the underside of the softwood bench peg. To discover if the point is ready for use, its sharpness can be judged by touching the cutting edge to the thumbnail. It should catch: if it skids off, the graver is not sharp enough and needs to be put back to the oilstone. For

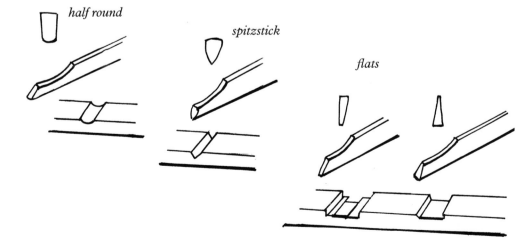

half round

spitzstick

flats

Scorpers.

more detailed information, see the excellent chapter in Oppi Untracht's book, *Jewellery, Concepts and Technology*.

Engraving for Champlevé

There are three key factors in successful engraving: patience, concentration and comfort. Above all else patience and experience are needed to achieve good results, and being in any hurry is fatal. You have to be able to sit quietly and concentrate without interruption for long periods of time, so a comfortable position, which will not put a strain on the neck and back, is essential. The metal to be engraved should be at a height where the elbows are supported on the bench and the shoulders are down and relaxed. Usually a prepared piece of wood covered with setter's wax and supported on a large sandbag is a sufficient prop, but you may need additional height.

Many professional engravers use an engravers' vice, which is an expensive piece of equipment, and not really necessary for the amount of time the enameller will spend engraving to begin with. Depending on the light source in the engraving position and your eyesight, you may need to use an illuminated magnifier or magnifying pair of goggles, which also protect the eyes.

Having decided on the design to be engraved and which areas are to be removed and subsequently enamelled, any findings that the piece requires should be soldered on before setting it into the setter's wax. The metal must be between 20 and 24 gauge to ensure that it will not warp in the kiln, unless of course the piece is going to be counter-enamelled (*see* Chapter 2). Once the metal has been gently warmed, placed in the setter's wax and cooled, it will be ready for the chosen design to be transferred. One of the simplest ways to transfer the design, either from a tracing of the design or freehand drawing, is to roll a piece of plasticine over the surface of the metal first, forming a light film which allows the graphite impression to show up

Engraving Safety

It is very important that all the cuts must be made **away** from the body, and it is sensible to wear a protector, such as a finger stall, on the finger of the hand that is holding the metal and is in direct line of the cuts being made.

clearly. Having established the design it is possible to make a more permanent mark through the plasticine film with a scriber or sharp point. It is generally agreed that it is easier to carve out one cell at a time if there are several in the design.

To begin the carving, use a half-round scorper No 6 to produce a cut just inside the scribed line. Your movements should be controlled, and short cuts made quite deeply all round, working from the outline of the area towards the centre of the cell. Once this metal is removed it will give a good indication of the depth being cut and you can repeat the procedure until the required depth is achieved. Great care must be taken when working at the edge of the design. It is not necessary to push too vigorously if the graver is sharp nor to attempt to get in the corners at this stage (*see* Oppi Untracht, *Jewellery, Concepts and Technology*).

The next move is to take out the areas within these initial cuts using a flat scorper No 8 or smaller, starting from the half-round cut work, pushing outwards and towards the middle of the cell. Repeat this process until the required depth is achieved (about 0.3mm). You can then switch to a wider scorper, No 14, to flatten the base and smooth it out by working in different directions. It is better to do more layers slowly in the beginning and to work logically, changing directions to ensure the levels go down evenly. Rub charcoal over the piece to show exactly which areas still need to be cut away. A spitzstick, a wide, boat-shaped graver, can be used to clear the corners and true up the

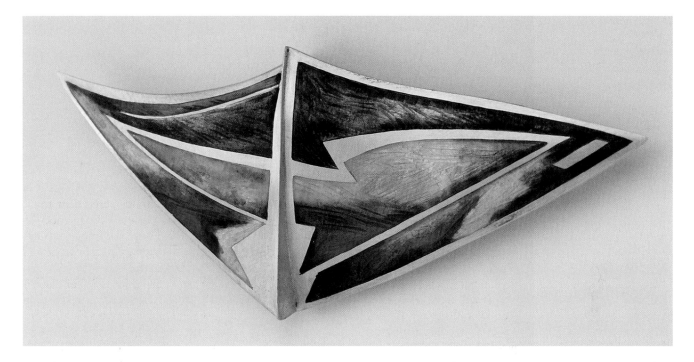

edges; sizes vary according to the manufacturer but a small one is acceptable to start
with. It is possible to lean out the edges
slightly at this time, which will prevent the
enamel from cracking.

When clearing the corner the first cut
should be from the point towards the
middle. Place the spitzstick in the corner
then lower your hand to make a controlled
push. If the corner needs to be wider,
return the spitzstick to its original position
and then turn it slightly to make a second
cut, repeating on the opposite side. Carry
on doing this until the corner is satisfactory, holding the spitzstick at a steeper
angle to clear the corner completely and
get more depth. Finally you can use the
spitzstick to neaten the outline, using the
side of the graver to clear where the metal
has not flicked out well enough.

The final depth needed is about 0.4mm;
if you go deeper than this difficulties will
arise when you start enamelling, but if your
cell is too shallow you will find that when
you have finished cleaning and polishing
the metal, there will be too little depth of

enamel. The other cells can now be carved
out in the same way. Once the carving is
complete, warm the piece slightly – more
than once if necessary – to remove the wax,
and then wipe the piece clean with tissue.

Cleaning
If standard silver is being used, rather than
pure or hardenable silver, you may have to
remove any oxide by immersing the piece
in a shallow dish of pure nitric acid. Add a
few drops of hot water, enough to just
raise the temperature, pour off the diluted
acid and brush off the darkened surface.
Then wash the silver again with a small
amount of nitric acid and finally brush
well under running water (*see* Chapter
10). However, as the piece has been
carved, the recesses should be oxide-free
and ready to fill with enamel, once the
piece has been degreased with hot soapy
water and ammonia. When clean it should
be wrapped in tissue and stored until it is
to be enamelled, but remember that the
results are much better if you enamel as
soon as possible after engraving.

*Brooch in silver
and champlevé.
Sarah Letts.*

Brooch in white and yellow gold with diamonds and aquamarine. Phil Barnes.

PHIL BARNES

Phil calls himself a second-generation en-ameller, as he worked as an apprentice to his father, C.F. Barnes, who started in the trade in 1926 and also taught enamelling part time at the Central School of Art and Craft from 1964 and at Sir John Cass School of Art. Phil watched his father at work from about eight years of age and started as an apprentice in 1967, attending evening classes in design and painting taught by George Lucas at the Cass. He believed it was a natural progression to follow in his father's footsteps as an enameller and worked with his father in the workshop in Great Queen Street in Holborn in London. In December 1962 he became a partner when the workshop moved to St John's Street in Clerkenwell. His father retired in 1983 and for a short time Phil continued the workshop with Alan Mudd (also a working partner), before leaving to set up his own premises, first in Clapham, where Sarah Wilson became his first apprentice, and later in Faygate, West Sussex, trading as Phil Barnes (Enameller).

Phil has earned the respect of the enam-elling fraternity and has achieved a special

Potpourri dish in silver and champlevé. Phil Barnes.

place in contemporary enamelling. He is highly regarded for his skills as a superb craftsman working on traditional pieces and his own innovative work, which he designs and makes for exhibition. He is also a dedicated and informed teacher and has been a visiting lecturer in enamelling and engraving at Sir John Cass College for over seventeen years, and given master classes in both England and America. Phil has won many awards since 1971 in the Goldsmiths Art Council Competition in the enamelling section, and he won the Jacques Cartier Craftsman of the Year Award in 1971. His enamelled pieces have been included in the Goldsmiths' Company travelling exhibition in Boston and San Francisco, and Frankfurt. He also exhibited at Limoges, France, in 1986 and 1990 and was a finalist in the Massana Soldevila Premi Internacional D'Esmalt, Barcelona, in 1987. He has work in the collection of the Musée l'Horologerie de Geneva. Phil was awarded the Freedom of the Goldsmiths' Company in 1978 and the Freedom of the City of London in the same year.

Phil heads a very successful enamelling workshop where the enamellers spend a large part of the daily work freelancing for designer craftsmen, goldsmiths, silversmiths and jewellers. The workshop also undertakes commissions from the retail trade and for both corporate and livery companies. At times Phil finds such commissions – and working closely with the clients' ideas and designs – restrictive, but the demands on the enamellers' skills can be taken as a challenge. He works only on precious metals and incorporates the colours of these metals with the brilliance of the enamels and engraving to give his pieces the quality unique to enamelling. Phil has recently made the decision to close his workshop in Faygate once Rachel Harvey finishes her apprenticeship with him, when he will set up a workshop in the garden of his London home to give himself time to concentrate on his personal work.

SARAH LETTS

Sarah originally trained at Chelsea School of Art as a printmaker and lithographer, but started enamelling after being introduced to it on an extended study course at Sir John Cass College. Sketchbooks and watercolour painting have always been important to Sarah, particularly as a starting point for her enamel design work. She uses sections of her paintings and abstracts them into enamel designs as brooches, earrings and pendants, the outline shape always enhancing the inner area of enamel. Sarah's thin layers of champlevé enamel give the appearance of soft, silky fabric, and the detail engraving beneath the enamel is reminiscent of shallow river beds, rocks, pebbles and gently running water. She says she is intrigued by the challenge of achieving the colours she needs, which often emerge from the kiln not quite as she expected, but still wonderful and always different. She says she is not a perfectionist and yet she is always hopeful that her next piece will be the one that meets all her criteria. She finds that:

...enamel has a mesmerizing hold on her creativity, and she uses silver as her canvas; the metal is striated, giving texture beneath the enamel; this enhances the colours and brings a particular depth to the work'
(From a statement about the artist for an exhibition.)

Recently Sarah has retired from teaching at Sir John Cass College and intends to spend more time experimenting with new ideas. She is a co-director of Studio Fusion and one of the first members of the British Society of Enamellers, with whom she has exhibited both nationally and internationally. Since 1996 she has had her work exhibited in New York and Seattle, Madrid and Barcelona, Ontario, and New Delhi and Bombay, as well as in many British venues.

Necklace in silver and champlevé with enamelled beads. 2000. Sarah Letts.

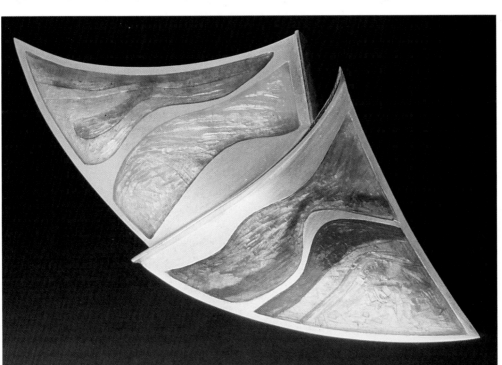

Brooch in silver, 18K yellow gold and champlevé. 2001. Sarah Letts.

Etching

Using an acid or mordant, the cells can be etched in order to receive the enamel for the inlay method. The piece of silver should be at least 16 gauge to ensure that the whole piece of metal is not weakened by the depth of the etch. Once the design has been prepared it can be transferred in the same way as described for the appliqué method (*see* page 57). When the line has been scribed, clean and degrease the surface of the metal ready to take some form of acid resist, which not only makes it easier to apply the resist but ensures a smooth result from the etch. If nitric acid is used as the etchant, possibly the best resist to employ is a 'stop-out', such as Rhinds Stop Out Varnish, which can be bought from graphic supply shops. Mask out the areas which will not be enamelled with varnish using a paintbrush, controlling the consistency of the varnish by thinning it slightly with drops of white spirit so that accurate lines can be achieved. Protect the reverse and edges of the piece with the stop-out, giving the varnish plenty of time to dry (usually about an hour) before starting a new process. The reverse side can be protected with candle grease or acid-resist tape; alternatively, if the silver is a thin gauge and needs to be counter-enamelled, you can do this before stopping out and etching as the acid will not harm the enamel.

Acid-resist tape (polyester silicone tape) can also be used to cover the entire surface and burnished down to make a good contact. With a sharp scalpel cut round the areas that are to be etched and remove these shapes, ensuring that the edges that are left are burnished down again so that they do not lift in the acid. The tape is a very easy way to protect the reverse side of the work, and there are specialist scalpels on the market with swivel heads, which facilitate cutting curves. If it is difficult to see the original lines of the design through the tape it may be necessary to ink the lines before applying the tape. The tape is also useful for sticking across the back of the piece to suspend it upside down in the acid and attach it to the sides of the acid container.

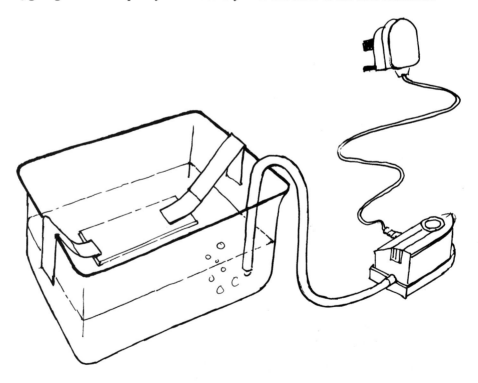

The acid bath.

The Acid Bath

When the metal is suspended upside down it tends to give a more even etch and it eliminates the need to brush away the gas bubbles which form on the surface of the metal when face up. These bubbles must be cleared, as they will otherwise pit the surface; use a feather to brush the metal. At the same time, it is useful to suspend a scrap piece of the same metal partly masked with tape, so it can be lifted occasionally to determine the depth of the etch.

It is possible to create a second or third level of etch if the piece is lifted out of the acid, gently brushed with warm soapy water and a small amount of ammonia to neutralize the acid. Dry the piece, stop out the areas that are to remain at the first level and replace it in the acid to eat down to a second level. If required a third level can be done in the same way. This multiple layering is, in effect, a rather simple form of bastaille enamelling in that varying depths and intensities of the same colour can be achieved, but there is no comparison with the lovely effects that engraving and chasing can give.

If ferric nitrate is used instead of nitric acid there are other methods of stopping out that can be used with great accuracy, such as a graphic white paint marker No 780 by Edding, permanent felt-tip pens and pens used for marking out circuit boards. Letraset can be interesting if used as part of a design, not as it comes straight off the sheet. Also contact fabrics such as Fablon can be cut and attached, but possibly only for largish objects. Ferric nitrate has an advantage over nitric acid in so far as it does not cause undercutting and gives sharp clear edges. However, for both acid and ferric nitrate the important point is that a slow etch is far the best; speeding the process can result both in losing the sharp edges and in undercutting. Different acids and mordants are used for gold and silver but the precautions are always the same when mixing and preparing the solutions (*see* Chapter 10).

A Brass Etching Unit to Stamp Cells

Originally champlevé enamel pieces were made by stamping recesses in the metal into which the glass was fused. An interesting contemporary development similar to this effect can be achieved by etching the negative of the design to be enamelled in a piece of brass. The etching process is identical to that already explained for silver and gold, in that the cleanliness and use of stop-out varnish or pens is the same. The only difference is the etching mordant: the etch for brass is one part ferric chloride to four parts distilled water.

The etch works faster if the solution is kept at a constant tepid temperature – placing the acid bowl into a bowl of warm water is a satisfactory method. The design is transferred to the brass; if you are making earrings or cufflinks you will have to etch two pieces, one the reverse of the other. Then stop out the design and put in the etch. Once the depth of etch is

---

Etching Acids for Silver and Gold

Strong solution	nitric acid 2 to 3 parts	distilled water 1 part
Weak solution	nitric acid 1 part	distilled water 3 to 5 parts
Ferric nitrate	1 part (soft crystals)	distilled water 4 parts
Aqua Regis	nitric acid 1 part	hydrochloric acid 3 parts
	distilled water 40 to 50 parts (this is very corrosive)	

NB Experience shows that the slower ferric nitrate etch gives a cleaner line, does not create undercuts and is pleasanter to use.

approximately 0.5mm, remove the brass and place it in hot soapy water and ammonia to neutralize the mordant and stop the etch continuing. To remove the stop-out use white spirit. With this mordant you can use all the acid-resist pens and so on described for use with ferric nitrate and silver.

Imprinting
The negative brass stamp is now ready to be pressed into the silver or gold. For ease and economy the size of the metal should be only slightly larger than the etched design on the brass. Flux and anneal the piece of silver or gold, clean in dilute sulphuric acid, rinse and dry. Place the two metals together, with the etched side down on to the precious metal, and bind together with regular lengths of tape to stop any movement. Take care to ensure that the taping is even and does not overlap, as this would give uneven pressures and spoil the imprint. Now place the item between two pieces of brass and pass it through the rolling mill with just enough pressure to impress the etched brass design into the silver without distorting the design. This will leave an impression deep enough to inlay a thin layer of enamel.

This method can be very effective when building up a three-dimensional and multi-layered piece of work, and it is also less wasteful than etching into gold. Before starting to lay in the enamel the piece must be thoroughly cleaned to remove any traces of the brass.

Designing for Photo-Etching
There are several variants of this technique for preparing silver for etching, a technique which is particularly suited to achieving limited runs of units or mass production of items which are to be enamelled. With carefully prepared artwork it is possible to achieve dozens of individual shapes from a relatively small sheet, interlocking the pieces to eliminate wastage of the metal and remembering to draw left and right designs for earrings and cufflinks. Each shape produced might be used as a single unit, or the pieces could be small parts of connecting units designed to create complex pieces of enamelled jewellery.

Brass etched (top left), silver stamped (right), and silver enamelled (bottom left). 2002. Jeanne Werge-Hartley.

Photo-Resist

A method that can be done on a small scale in a very basic workshop uses the same technique developed by the computer industry to make circuit boards, so you will need to acquire a photo-resist spray or liquid and a photo-resist developer from a circuit board distributor (Maplins). The artwork must be drawn up to be as black as possible on a white ground, the black areas being the parts that remain and the white parts being etched away to hold the enamel. The individual units should be cut out and re-mounted on a black ground, interlocking the shapes to reduce waste. Transfer the artwork to a piece of acetate by using a laser photocopier, available at most good stationers or graphic suppliers. This process should ensure that the black areas are impenetrable to light, but it is advisable to hold the photocopy transparency up to the light to check for pinholes. These can be covered with black ink. In your first experiments it is advisable to keep the transparency to a reasonably small size, as even on a 6 × 4cm area it is possible to etch out a substantial number of pieces by carefully interlocking the shapes.

Transferring the Design to the Metal

To ensure that the acid-resist adheres to the metal, the metal must be made totally clean and grease free by vigorously rubbing with pumice slurry until the water runs off in one sheet. Give the piece of silver a light-sensitive coating of photo-resist in subdued light, away from sources of UV light. It is best to work in a photographic dark room with a red safe light or contrive a similar environment. Spray the surface evenly with the resist and dry the plate at 50°C (122°F) for twenty minutes, either in a drying cupboard or with a hairdryer. Alternatively, let it dry naturally in a well-ventilated dark area for twelve hours. This procedure is known as the pre-bake. Keep the sensitized silver away from daylight by storing it in a light-proof container.

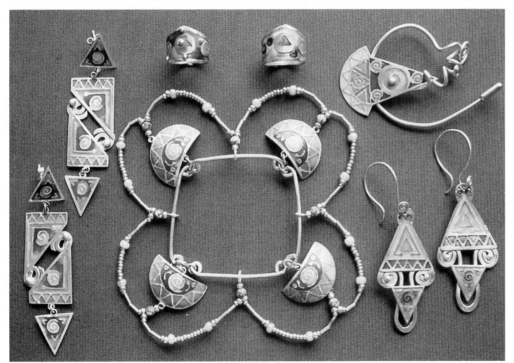

A collection of photo-etched jewellery. Ailsa Fishwick (student).

The next step, while still working in the red light, is to place the transparency in contact with the metal, and lay a piece of glass over it, both to keep it flat and to secure it. The metal and transparency should now be exposed to either bright daylight or an ultraviolet light (sun lamp) for one to five minutes depending on the strength of the light source – you should carry out controlled experiments to determine the optimum exposure for particular equipment.

Photo-etching equipment.

  PRP positive photo-resist

2 *PRP photo-resist developer*

3 *Glass hinged lid over wooden back to hold transparency over silver when exposing it to light*

4 *Transparency over silver sheet*

Photo-etching (detail).

1 *Acetate laser-printed with art work*

2 *Silver coated with PRP*

3 *Photo-etched leaves and flowers*

4 *Flower enamelled*

After the exposure is complete cover the piece with a very dark cloth to stop any further exposure and mix the developer at room temperature in a shallow dish. Remove the transparency and slip the exposed silver into the developer as quickly as possible. Gently agitate the developer by rocking the dish until the exposed green resist disappears, leaving the shapes that were protected from the light as dark green. Remove the silver as soon as the development is complete and leave for about thirty minutes in a warm place for the resist to harden – this is called the post-bake. Once the reverse and edges of the piece are protected by acid-resist tape, stop-out varnish or resist pen, it can be placed in the etching acid.

Using PnP Blue Etching Resist Film

This is a more accurate process than painting out a design with stop-out varnish and is much more economical than photo-etching when only small quantities are required. The preparation consists of taking an original high-contrast black and white drawing, remembering that the black areas will become the acid-resist parts and will remain as the raised metal design. Leave a few millimetres of black edge round the design so that in the transfer process the image will be well anchored. Feed the PnP film through a plain paper copier or laser printer so that the image will be printed on to the emulsion (dull) side.

Remember that when the film is applied to the metal the image is reversed, so for example lettering should be designed backwards. The copying machine should be set to maximum contrast and in some cases the machine may also need a backing sheet of plain paper.

To transfer the image onto the metal, place the film emulsion side down on the piece of metal, which must be oxide- and grease-free. Place the metal on an insulating surface, such as a piece of wood, and use an iron set at 'cotton' (or 'dry' if you are using a steam iron). Initially, tack the edges of the blue film with the iron by working outwards from the centre. Then use circular movements to transfer the image from the edges towards the middle.

BELOW LEFT: Etching a line for saw piercing.

BELOW: Necklace of cast units hung with etched silver and enamelled leaves and flowers. 1991. Jeanne Werge-Hartley.

Working with PnP film.

ABOVE

1. *Photocopied drawing on to acetate*
2. *Design on acetate photocopied on to PnP film*
3. *PnP transferred on to silver sheet, ready to etch*
4. *PnP after the transfer of images*

RIGHT

1. *Original drawing.*
2. *Drawing photocopied on to acetate*
3. *Acetate image photocopied on to PnP*
4. *Etched sheet silver*
5. *Fish sawn out and enamelled*

Within a few seconds the image should start to appear more pronounced through the film. The exact time it takes to transfer the entire image will depend on a number of things, including the type and thickness of metal, the density of the black image and the type of toner in the copier. As an example, a 75mm square of silver 1mm thick might take approximately five minutes.

Once the image appears dense black rather than blue when seen through the film, the metal should be cooled on a metal block. Using a fingernail or scalpel, gently peel away the film at the edge to check that the image is totally transferred. Always leave the centre of the design attached to assist re-registration if necessary, but when you are certain peel the film off. If any thin lines have spread or moved into clear areas, often because of excessive heating, they can be scraped back with a pin or scalpel and broken areas can be retouched with a stop-out. It is better to use a slow etch and a weaker solution to conserve the resist; after the etching the film can be removed with acetone or Polycleanse.

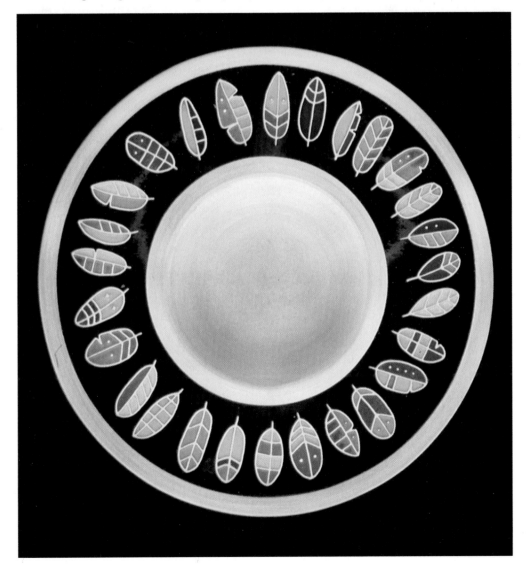

Brooch in photo-etched silver and enamel. Jane Moore.

Artwork prepared for photo-etching, with inset detail of red where the etch will go only half-way through the metal. Julie Sharpe (student).

DETAIL OF DRAWING
SHEET SHOWING THE
THE RED AREAS WHICH
WILL BE ETCHED ON
ONE SIDE ONLY, THE
BLACK LINES WILL
ETCH THROUGH TO
RELEASE THE PIECES

Industrial Photo-Etching

There are firms that will undertake the photo-etching process and, using original artwork, produce sheets of precious metal units for champlevé purposes. This method can be used for mass production or production runs of repeating multiples. With imaginative design work a number of ideas and items of differing sizes, complexity and variety can be arranged on the same artwork. The potential for an exciting and innovative collection of rings, earrings, necklaces and most other kinds of jewellery is enormous. Larger items such as cutlery, napkin rings and so on are all feasible as long as the gauge of the metal is suitable for the scale.

Design and Etching

The artwork you supply to the firm, for example Micrometallic Ltd, should be at least double the size of the finished pieces. This allows the detail to be drawn accurately and mistakes that would ultimately

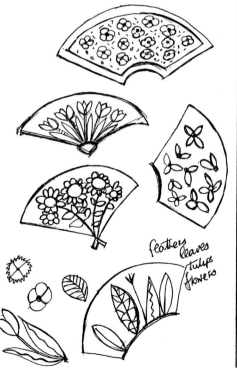

Sketchbook drawings. Jane Moore.

cause problems in the etching process to be identified. The artwork is reduced photographically by Micrometallic to the required size before processing, which also refines the detail.

Drawings for the photo-etching process should be produced in black and red on white. The artwork is done as one sheet of drawing, and the dividing of the colours is done by a colour separation camera at Micrometallic. The red parts are transferred to the top side of the metal sheet, allowing the etch to go halfway through to make the recesses, while the black lines and areas are used on both sides of the sheet of metal to allow the etch to penetrate all the way through, eliminating the need to saw out the pieces. This method can be very useful to produce a variety of small parts that can then be added to a larger composite piece, and relieves the tedium of sawing out lots of small units. Blue is sometimes introduced into the art work to allow optional additional etching

Brooches in photo-etched silver and enamel. Jane Moore.

Detail of artwork, photo-etched piece and finished piece. Jane Moore.

to take place on the reverse of the sheet, for example the maker's name or distinguishing pattern or marks. The resist is photographed on to the metal and the piece is sprayed from both sides with acid in a controlled situation.

According to Micrometallic there is no standard size required but they recommend, as an economical size, final artwork measuring 160 × 29mm to be used on a piece of metal 185 × 35mm. It is advisable to telephone and discuss your ideas with them before you start.

Preparation and Enamelling
Findings such as brooch or earring fittings should be soldered on before cleaning and polishing; medium solder can be used as these parts can be protected by Diewersol or a similar paste while in the kiln. After cleaning in the pickle the piece should be hand polished to eliminate any scratches and marks on the metal surrounds and then cleaned in hot soapy water and ammonia to eliminate any dirt or grease that would contaminate the enamel (*see* Chapter 3). Having prepared the enamel by grinding and washing (*see* Chapter 2), place the piece of metal on a grid of iron mesh which has been bent round at the edge to raise it off the kiln floor about 2cm. If the piece has findings soldered on to the reverse it is vital to protect these by covering them with the Diewersol, which also helps to balance the piece. As an alternative there is a heat-reflective ceramic fibreboard on the market, which will allow the findings to be pressed into the soft texture and keep the piece level. This fibre material is also excellent when using other enamelling techniques, such as plique à jour, and when making repairs.

If pure or hardenable silver is used firestain is not a problem; other metals can be coated with FM flux solution, which, if allowed to dry, will help to decrease the amount of firestain forming in the kiln. The solution should not be applied where it will come in contact with the enamel. When the final layer of enamel has been fired, the piece must be stoned with different materials, from abrasive carborundum sticks down to very fine emery paper boards. Water may be used with all the abrasives but not with the emery papers unless they are silicon carbide. Once the enamel is flush with the surrounding metal any pinholes or blemishes can be rectified using a fine drill in a holder, refilled and fired again. Before the holes are refilled the piece must be well cleaned, either by brushing with pumice powder under running water or placing in a small ultrasonic bath with warm, soapy water for about three minutes and then rinsing well under running water.

Finishing
There are four ways of finishing the enamel, each one as interesting as the others. Flash firing done in a fast, hot kiln brings the enamel back to a gloss finish. Alternatively, once it has been flash fired and you are sure it is entirely free of pinholes or cracks, you can achieve a matt surface by rubbing with silicon carbide papers wrapped round a piece of wood (an old emery stick is ideal). The wood keeps the paper as flat as possible while a fair amount of pressure is applied. Using increasingly finer papers and changing direction each time the paper is changed make the scratch marks gradually finer and finer. Depending on the quality of the finish required other abrasives can be used, such as fine pumice powder (240 mesh) mixed with water and liquid soap.

Matting Salts Solution

(*See* Useful Addresses: Vitrum Signum) Immersion for one to five minutes produces a frosted matt finish to the enamel without being too damaging to the metal.

To achieve an eggshell finish once the matt finish has been reached, continue rubbing with a Water of Ayr stone, felt, or leather buff sticks charged with wet rouge powder. The rouge powder should be used very sparingly, particularly if white or pale colours are involved. The best results, needless to say, come with a great deal of elbow grease and patience.

The fourth finish is not often used today but can be incorporated in a piece to imitate gemstones such as turquoise and carnelian. In the last firing the enamel is piled high in the centre of the cell and will be left in relief when it is fired. This method has the intriguing name of 'En Grotte de Suif', meaning tallow drops.

As long as the metal is continually protected, kept free from scratches and the solder kept to a minimum, the final cleaning and polishing can be simplified. The finished article will have a professional appearance of not being overworked – not having sharp edges rounded and not having areas of firestain spoiling the lustre of the polish.

JANE MOORE

Jane Moore is recognized as one of the foremost British enamellers using the method of photo-etching. She produces a very wide range of colourful production jewellery and small pictures, which all have a distinctive personal design quality that is recognizably Jane's.

Jane was trained in the Jewellery and Silversmithing department of Loughborough College of Art and Design. She is a full member of the British Society of Enamellers and joined the Designer Jewellers Group in 1999, exhibiting with the Group in the Barbican and the touring exhibition, Celebration. Other exhibitions include Contemporary Enamels at the Bilston Craft Gallery, the Goldsmiths' Hall Fair in 1999 and 2000 and three Chelsea Craft Fairs. Her work is in many collections, including Birmingham City and Liverpool Art galleries. Jane has recently opened her own gallery, called Contemporary Jewellery, in Leamington Spa.

Collection of photo-etched, enamelled jewellery. Jane Moore.

Jane writes of her work: 'The inspiration for my jewellery often derives from creatures and flowers both real and imaginary which are depicted in the art of ancient cultures.' She designs in her sketchbook and has a notebook of ongoing ideas from which she aims to make a new collection each spring. To develop her drawings she constructs card mock-ups in three dimensions and, when she has refined the idea, she draws up the designs using OHP projector pens on non-absorbent card and has photocopies made using a laser copier. The master patterns are pasted onto card and photo-etched commercially to 0.3mm in silver. The individual units are sawn from the silver sheets, then assayed and hallmarked before cleaning and shaping in a hydraulic press. After more cleaning the pieces are enamelled, the findings soldered on and the pieces finally polished.

OPPOSITE PAGE: Bird shadow bowl (18.5cm) in silver, champlevé and basse taille.

BELOW: Bird shadow bowl (detail).
Jane Short.

BASSE TAILLE ENAMELLING

Definition and History

Basse taille is the shortened form of the French name *émail en basse taille*. It applies to all enamelling over a surface that has been carved, chased or patterned in any way, such as low relief, intaglio and repoussé on gold and silver. Sometimes it is difficult to make an absolute distinction between champlevé and basse taille, as, for example, when the ground has been decorated and transparent enamel has been used as opposed to the opaque enamel usually used in champlevé. An example of this was Guilloche, introduced in the nineteenth century, in which engine-turned patterns were created to give transparent enamels extra brilliance. This is still used today on cufflinks and box lids.

According to Labarte, enamel over silver relief was first mentioned in 1286, when it was apparently used in a high altar made by John of Pisa for Bishop Guglielmino Ubertini of Arezzo. However, the earliest existing example of this art form is a gold chalice made by Guccio Di Mannaia of Sienna for the Convent of St Francis of Assisi in 1290. Throughout the Renaissance period the luminosity and light-reflective effect of basse taille enamelling had great symbolic importance, and the technique was used to decorate such large religious objects as silver candelabras and reliquaries. Sadly, very few pieces remain from the vast number of articles made during the Renaissance period and most of the ones that have survived are held in cathedrals and churches. A wonderful treasure held in the British Museum, known as 'The Royal Gold Cup of the Kings of England and France', illustrates the legend of St Agnes. The cup was made in Paris between 1380 and 1390 for Charles V in basse taille on gold.

Cellini, in his sixteenth-century treatise on goldsmithing, writes about intaglio worked into metal to the depth of 'two ordinary sheets of paper', and he was insistent about the use of the chisel and engravers to give good definition to the chased detail.

A Macaroni 'Chatelaine' in blue enamel over engine turning, with diamonds and gold stars edged with pearls. (In the collection of Genevieve E. Cummins.) James Shrapnell.

Beaker (7.5cm diameter) in silver, champlevé and basse taille. Jane Short.

Today there are true experts in this field: for example, Alan Mudd is able to cut so accurately that although his deepest cut may only be fifteen thousandths of an inch (0.38mm) deep, there can be as many as fifteen to twenty varying levels in the same piece.

The techniques for engraving for champlevé apply equally to basse taille. However, you do need to use more refined methods to prepare the metal for enamelling with basse taille work. Engraving and carving the varying depths of the recesses for the low relief or intaglio takes time, patience and great skill, and, to produce a piece of merit, an innate sense of design is vital.

Enamelling after Carving

Having carved the piece it is better to enamel the metal as soon as possible while it is bright and oxide-free, especially if standard silver is being used. Wash the piece well in running water and dry with a clean tissue.

Only the most translucent enamels are used for basse taille to cover the bas relief with a uniform coating, allowing the modelled surface to give the variations of tone with a single colour. The aim is to have as thin a layer of glaze as possible so that the light falling on the enamel passes through and reflects back from the gold or silver base. Depending on the depth of the carving either one or two layers are sufficient – the first one just covering the highest point of the carving and the second refilling the shrinkage of the first layer if necessary – as too thick a depth of glass will produce a heavy and unpleasant effect, hiding the delicate detailing of the design. Where the modelling is shallower the colour will be paler than in the deeper recesses, giving the illusion of shading.

A unique effect, only possible with this technique, is to create a translucent picture by laying and firing different colours next to each other to emphasize the carved design. When filing and hand finishing the piece, care must be taken not to cut through the enamel and risk damaging the carving.

Often a thin top layer of flux is fired over the whole piece for protection, which can increase the translucency if the flux is minimally thicker in the centre and the carving and engraving can be seen more clearly.

Many enamellers today are producing basse taille pieces as interest in this intriguing ancient craft grows. There are many very competent craftsmen in the trade who work to other people's designs and also pass on their knowledge to students in the art colleges. There are a few artist craftsmen who have taken this particular aspect of enamelling further and have produced work of exceptional quality.

JANE SHORT

Jane has become one of Britain's foremost artist enamellers and, like other great enlightened designer craftsmen before her, has chosen to pass on her knowledge and expertise to others through her teaching commitments. Her own work is made with sensitivity and a subtlety of shape and colour that is very personal and recognizable. Basse taille and champlevé enamelling have become her usual methods although initially she was known for her cloisonné work.

Jane trained at the Central School of Arts and Crafts, where she later returned to teach part time from 1979, and influenced Fred Rich to start his enamelling career. After leaving the Central School, she went to the Royal College of Art, where she received her MA in jewellery and enamelling. She established her own workshop in 1979, not only making her own enamel silver jewellery but also undertaking to enamel the work of Leo De Vroomen, Roger Doyle and Clive Burr.

Jane says that she has been fascinated by the possibilities in the technique of enamelling since she was first introduced to it by Pat Furze at the Central School in 1974, and has produced enamel silverware and jewellery ever since. She sees her work as a continual exploration into the possibilities of the wonderful range of colours available to her. In some pieces she is interested in the soft subtle harmonies of colour reflecting observations of nature, at other times the richness and vibrancy of colour provokes a more personal imagery.

Jane's current work combines the techniques of engraving and carving, which she learnt to do mainly through experience at the Royal College of Art, followed by some specific advice on carving from Phil Barnes. Enamelling in the methods of basse taille and champlevé, she engraves out the background and then carves detailed patterns that show through the transparent enamel and produce a rich but subtle painterly effect, as in her feather brooches. Jane is currently exploring the potential of leaving areas of carved metal contrasting with areas of enamel. This approach can be seen to best advantage in the Millennium Plate commissioned by the Worshipful Company of Goldsmiths to feature in a major exhibition, called Treasures of the Twentieth Century, which took place during May and July 2000. It was one of a number of pieces the Company commissioned from eminent British craftsmen.

Cloisonné silver brooch. 2002. Jane Short.

The Millennium Plate

Jane's description of the making of this beautiful plate is very instructive, not only with regard to the manufacture of the piece and the enamelling process, but in the way it shows how a master designer craftsman identifies and solves the problems inherent in this particular technique. She started sketching ideas, well aware of all the problems a large piece can pose for the enameller. Her main design element revolved around the sense of our time, our place in the universe and the celebration of our existence. Her idea was to make the piece in two parts: the inner area of the plate was to be rich in colour and detail and the outer deep rim was to be mainly engraved and lightly hammered at the edge. The spiral motif refers both to the patterns that the smallest particles of energy can make, and to the spirals seen in the patterns of the galaxies. The definite division between the inner and outer parts of the bowl is linked by the spiral. The blue outer swirl represents water and the

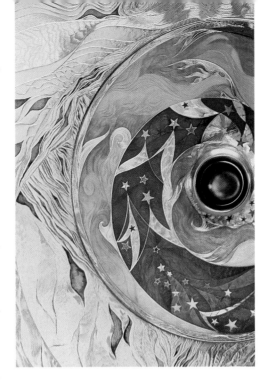

Millennium Plate (detail), in engraved silver and champlevé. Jane Short.

inner swirl the night sky with all the stars and fireworks motifs. The yellow area represents rock turning to fire, celebratory beacon bonfires and the earth's molten core. The spiral vanishes into the centre of the plate, the black hole, which is a reminder of the vastness of space and the celebration of our existence in space.

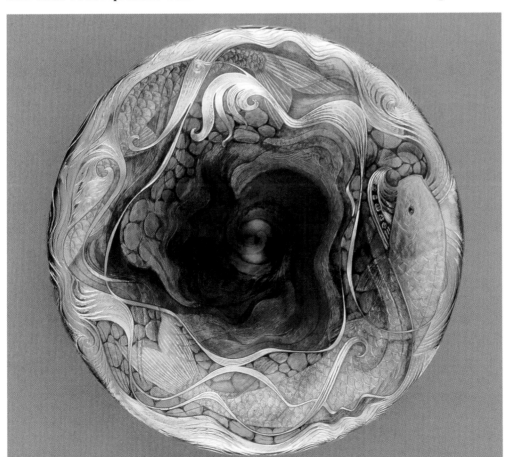

Bowl (18.5cm) in silver, champlevé and basse taille. 2001. Jane Short.

Although Jane makes her own jewellery, her silverware is made up in Clive Burr's workshop. Once the design for the Millennium Plate was approved by Rosemary Ransome-Wallis of Goldsmiths' Hall, Jane visited Clive Burr and they discussed the making process and all the problems that had to be overcome. In order to accommodate this large plate Jane had to purchase a larger kiln, the performance of which was an additional concern. Once the silversmithing was completed Jane settled to many hours of engraving and carving, something which she enjoys. She says that she loves the rhythm associated with the process of carving and enamelling.

She had concerns when she came to the enamelling process, which can easily be understood as the enamel colours can change so much in a single firing from what the enameller imagined. The laying-in of enamel in such large areas, such as the blue and yellow spiral, requires the utmost concentration with no interruptions. The other difficulty encountered in laying enamels into such a large piece is to remember exactly where each colour is. As Jane explains, pinks, reds, oranges, yellows and clear fluxes look so similar to each other and nothing like their final colour before they are fired. This concentration is also an exercise in trying to imagine what the final effect will be, and she says that this is the time when she is most focused on the exact colour going where and with what, and when her final decisions have to be made.

The sheer size of the plate gave rise to the problem of how to make sure the kiln was hot enough so that the enamels fired and stayed their true colour, but not so hot that the solder seams would deteriorate or the plate itself distort. She made a framework out of ceramic fibreboard to support the piece, and she comments how beneficial this space-age material is to shape customized supports for items to be fired, as it does not move in the kiln or absorb too much heat. The new kiln, made by David Alexander to Jane's specifications, proved to be good once she had become accustomed to it, and she finds that it does not lose too much heat when the door is opened, which ensures an even firing of the enamel. She also says that possibilities have begun to open up regarding the scale of her work. Having to resort to using a garden spade to move the piece in and out of the kiln due to its weight and size illustrates just one of the problems of working to this scale.

Enamelling the outer rim was less complex as there was less enamel to apply. Most of the engraving on this outer rim was done before the enamelling was complete, with the final details around the enamelled areas being engraved last of all, just before the final firing. Finally the two parts were fitted together and glued to complete the piece.

In an article that Jane wrote for *The Goldsmiths' Gazette* after she had finished the Millennium commission she says:

> The process of enamelling starts with careful preparation of metals and enamels; continues with an extremely focused period when the enamel is laid; the telling moments of firing the piece in the kiln to reveal its true colour; the adding of more enamel in successive fired layers; the final rubbing back and refiring of the enamel; and ends with finishing off the metal to complete the piece. It has, like all making processes, its own rhythm of careful planning and preparation, concentration and focus, observation and attention to detail, which hopefully culminates in a piece that fulfils one's hopes and desires.

Jane goes on to explain how, having channelled so much of her energy into the project over many months, all the different processes clouded her view of the piece for a time, despite her relief at completing the commission and the excitement of seeing her designs come to fruition. However, as she took the plate out of its box at

Goldsmiths' Hall she was pleased to find that she 'rather liked it'.

From the beginning of the commission Jane's premise was to enjoy making this piece and her enjoyment is evident in the result. The final assembled magnificent plate proved to be far greater than the sum of its parts and expresses Jane's intuitive design sense coupled with her supreme craftsmanship.

Jane seems to manage a similar 'rhythm' to her life as she combines her talent as a master designer enameller with not only producing work for commissions, exhibitions, some teaching, and enamelling other silversmiths' pieces, but also exploring all the new possibilities of working with precious metals, enamels and fire in her own innovative, distinctive and superb way.

FRED RICH

Fred Rich is possibly one of Britain's most exciting and talented designer enamellers. His work is in great demand and held in many international collections. Because of the complexity of his pieces and the time-consuming techniques that he employs, each piece often takes months of intense and arduous work and it is not surprising that there is a queue of collectors and clients eagerly waiting to commission their pieces, which are not only hall-marked and have his registered letters (FR), but often also carry a signature. The personal mark FR has changed since 2000 and is now FRED (Fred Rich Enamel Designs).

When working with a client he takes pleasure in talking about the personal touches that he can bring to each piece, which makes each item very special to that person and something to be treasured for the future. It is obvious when talking to him that experimenting with colour and achieving depth and brilliance in his pieces is of the utmost importance, and he feels that enamel allows him this wonderful and glowing palette.

After leaving school Fred took a series of jobs, but by chance became interested in jewellery and started taking evening classes with Tom Saddington. During this time he was persuaded to apply to the Central School of Arts and Crafts in London, and was accepted on the foundation course in

Butterfly Vase, commissioned by the Worshipful Company of Goldsmiths. 1996. Fred Rich.

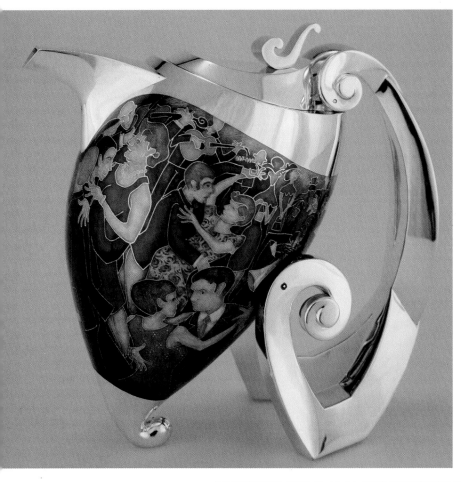

ABOVE: Tea Dance teapot. 1998. Fred Rich.

1977. This all-encompassing year provided him with a sound basis for his future design work, and he says that it really opened his eyes as his previous education had been rather academic. He resisted the tutors' advice to take his degree in painting and sculpture because, although he had not had the opportunity to make any jewellery in this first year, he was determined to enter the jewellery course.

His jewellery tutors at the Central School proved to be very influential in his future, and he remembers his head of department, Brian Wood, tutors Kevin Coates and Pat Furze (who introduced him to enamelling), and Jane Short, who tutored him in his third year. Fred, ever eager to acquire more skills, took evening classes in specialist techniques such as engraving and diamond setting, and went on to win a Diamonds International Award in 1988 and a Gold-smiths' Craft Council Award in 1994.

Leaving college with a first-class Honours degree in 1981, he set up in a work-shop shared with two other ex-students of Central, Annabel Ely and Tom McEwan. During this time he used his skills as an enameller to decorate other craftsmen's pieces, including the work of Leo De

Tea Dance cream and sugar. 2000. Fred Rich.

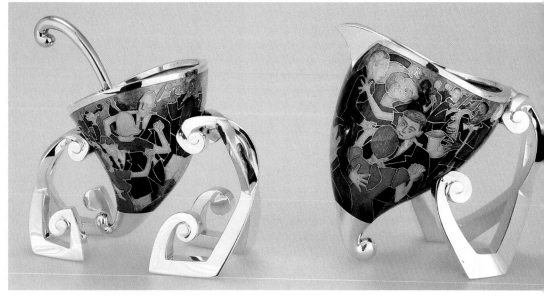

spontaneous attitude to his designs is often unexpected, as is his ability to surprise in making unusual and asymmetric shapes. This is something Fred's admirers have come to look forward to and admire in his current work, as demonstrated by his jewellery in the Goldsmiths' four-man show, Rising Stars.

His work is inspired by nature – everything from flowers, birds, fish and insects to the human figure. Fred's humorous, beautifully perceived and executed Tea Dance teapot set in 1998 is a delight. His candlesticks, made in 1996 for Garrards, have their bases deliciously enamelled with a bosomly lady playing the piano and a selection of other musicians playing violins and harps. He constantly develops sketchbooks of the images he sees around him, including a collection of beetles and butterflies he found on the Isle of Wight. When one customer commissioned a vase based on his own garden pond, Fred included in the design flora and fauna from the pond, specific fish, the client's bird table perched over an island, and his resident kingfisher, which gave the vase its name. This piece won the Jacques Cartier Award in 1996.

LEFT: Musicians' Candlesticks. 1996. Fred Rich.

BELOW: Musicians' Candlesticks (detail). Fred Rich.

Vroomen and Stephen Webster. Having started to get some recognition through winning awards at college, he began to receive commissions from Sotheby's, the World Gold Council and the British Museum. De Beers bought one of his necklaces for the trainer of the winning horse for the George VI Diamond Stakes in July 1984, and he subsequently went on to make the Diamond Stakes Trophy in 1988.

After a few years in London in his Portobello Green workshop he moved to Surrey. He says that he is surprised that he has had to do so little to promote his work, but his reputation for quality enamelling and his friendly and confident nature ensure a steady flow of potential clients and commissions. Fred's ever-changing and

A change in direction came about in an association with Garrards after one of Fred's beakers had been displayed in an exhibition, Royal Goldsmiths, at Garrards in 1993. Through the support of Richard Jarvis of Garrards, Ann Weston and Corrina Pyke, who is one of Fred's greatest admirers, a one-man show was proposed in 1995. This was to be the first time Fred tackled the large enamelled objects for which he is now so well known. Much of the work was experimental, and he admits that the learning curve was steep. His method of construction changed and was adapted to the need for continual firings and the limitations that this imposed on both the shape and the form of the silver. He is still experimenting with his adaptations, as any craftsman of his calibre will do, pushing the boundaries and surprising his admirers again and again.

The one-man show at Garrards was hugely successful and a complete sell-out.

In 1996, to celebrate this show, the Worshipful Company of Goldsmiths commissioned a silver and gilt enamel vase involving basse taille and 22K gold cloisonné enamels. In this piece Fred created the illusion of a secret garden in which painted lady and red admiral butterflies hover and settle on young green ivy leaves, while between the leaves the subtle feline features of a stone leopard peer out rather menacingly. In 1991 this beautiful vase won all the sections for which it was entered in the Goldsmiths' Craft Council Competition. Fred also won the Jacques Cartier Memorial Award for the Craftsman of the Year with another piece.

A combination of basse taille and cloisonné enamelling techniques are used in nearly all his work. The cloisonné wires are soldered to the base and then the metal is carved and engraved. Once the piece is prepared, the painstaking laying-in of the enamels is started and it is interesting to

note that Fred grinds and mixes his enamels as a painter mixes his colours to achieve exactly the hue and tone of colour he needs. Because of the varying depths of enamel on the carved areas, and the range of the firing times of individual colours, the overall firing times are critical. He has to keep a very tight balance between the requirements of the different enamels to keep the piece in the kiln for the right time and at the correct temperature. The initial firings are quick, but the final ones are critical, and calculating exactly the right moment to remove a piece from the kiln is an enameller's nightmare.

Fred maintains that his show at Garrards gave him greater momentum and resulted in a change of pace in his work, which has allowed him more freedom to design and change his ways of making. He says that he became more focused and was able from that time to put out the silversmithing side of his work to Andrew Metcalfe and other specialists when the need arose. Currently silversmith Tim Chilcott is working with him, which presumably allows him the time to concentrate fully on his enamelling. He acknowledges the support he received from Garrards and is full of praise for the staff who worked there at that time.

Fred has recently won his second Jacques Cartier Award and a number of other awards in the Goldsmiths' Crafts Council Competition 2001, for a Millennium Vase for the Ironmongers Company. As the base of the piece he used three salamanders, emblematic of the Ironmongers, holding up a fiery crucible from which the flames lick up around the vase and flow into the enamelled design, with sparks extending into the night sky to become stars. The cyclical nature of time is represented by four floral panels, which billow up from the flames and represent the four seasons. These extend into the top piece of the vase, which also incorporates other elements associated with the Ironmongers' coat of arms.

5 CLOISONNE

DEFINITION AND HISTORY

Examples of cloisonné enamel have survived for thousands of years with the colours as beautiful as when the pieces were made. The cloisons are rectangular thin wires, which, when attached to a base, enclose areas called cells, into which the ground coloured glass is fused. Not only do these wires outline the design and contain the colours, but they also protect the enamel from damage.

Cloisonné is the oldest form of enamelling. The goldsmiths of more than 4,000 years ago used cloisons but only as a method of enclosing gemstones and pastes, such as Egyptian paste, which were cold cemented into the cells. It was not until the Mycenaean period (around 1450 BC) that coloured glass was fused into the metal cells. Greek jewellers in the sixth century BC also used fused enamels set into delicate filigree wires.

It was in the Byzantine period that cloisonné enamel developed into a stylized and complex figurative art form. At the climax of the Byzantine period, between the ninth and the twelfth centuries AD, their enamels were made on small, thin gold plaques and were designed for inclusion into larger objects, typical subject matter being saints and other religious figures. Smaller versions of these inserts, which decorated head-dresses and jewellery, were a kind of micro-cloisonné. The rich and colourful Byzantine style of cloisonné influenced other forms of enamelling in

Beads Blackfoot and Zuni, two-sided 'rocks' of fine silver, gold and cloisonné. Alexandra Raphael.

Brooch in hardenable silver, 18K gold and cloisonné. 1998. Jeanne Werge-Hartley.

the following years but the use of gold was rare elsewhere. It seems that champlevé on copper gilt replaced cloisonné in western European workshops. However, in central and eastern European countries, where the Byzantine influences held, silver filigree styles developed.

Cloisonné enamelling was used extensively in China from the sixteenth century, but only in decoration on copper vases and other large vessels, not on precious metals nor for items associated with body adornment. It was also used by Japanese enamellers in the nineteenth and twentieth centuries. It is still the most popular enamelling method in the Far East today and is seen by the general public as being a Far Eastern technique.

It was not until the nineteenth century that cloisonné appeared again in the West in a resurgence of interest, initially in Byzantine artefacts, which gave rise to great interest in the manufacture of fakes. New work, influenced by Japanese design, was produced in France, principally by the jeweller Falize. It was the art enamellers of the nineteenth century who brought the cloisonné technique to the fore and started to use this old and beautiful technique both for jewellery and for large panels.

CLOISONNE TECHNIQUES

Making Cloisonné Wires

Although cloisonné wire may be bought commercially in 1oz reels, it can be made in the workshop by drawing 1mm wire through a fine round or square draw plate to about 0.4mm, and then making it rectangular by putting it through a rolling mill. The wires may be standard, Britannia, pure or hardenable silver. Many of the karat golds may be used but the most used is 18K yellow. Platinum needs very special care (*see* Chapter 3).

Normally the wires are rectangular and between 0.2mm and 0.3mm thick, and 1.5–1.8mm high and fixed vertically to the base, although round wire can be used. Filigree wire is made by twisting two fine wires evenly and then gently flattening

Variations of cloisonné wire thicknesses.

them through the rollers and again fixing vertically so that a decorative edge shows against the enamel.

The wires may also be forged to form interesting line variations. The wires do not necessarily have to be the same thickness; if the design requires a variation of line any width can be used.

Forming the Wires

Before shaping the wires in any way it is important to anneal them, and this is best done in a coil to prevent melting. Curves should be shaped, preferably between the fore finger and the thumb, or by holding the end of the wire in pliers and shaping with the fingers. The wires should not be shaped by the pliers as this will mark the delicate wire and is unlikely to produce such sweet curves.

Fixing the Wires

There are two schools of thought today about the construction of cloisonné. Some enamellers prefer to make their cloisons and lay them into a thin layer of flux, which, when fired, will keep the wires secure until subsequent colours are laid in and fired. Another variation of this method is to fire a thin layer of flux and then position the wires on top of the flux with gum tragacanth or Klyrfyre and refire, allowing the wires to sink into the

flux. This works well on a very free abstract design and pieces where the cloisons are used solely to hold the enamel on to the metal rather than to separate the colours – for example, where the colour blends across the piece and shades into various tones and hues.

The second method is to solder the cloisons to the base, which ensures that they cannot move at all during packing or firing. This is particularly important with a complex design. Soldering the cloisons can be difficult for people less experienced in metal techniques, but hopefully the following notes will be useful.

Soldering the Wires

When the wires are to go on to a flat base they should be shaped individually over the drawing or design, then, when the network is complete, placed on the soldering block with a very small piece of enamelling solder under each point where the wires meet. Flux, then gently heat and solder the wires together. This should allow enough solder to also fix the series of wires to the base plate. If the wires are absolutely flat to the clean and fluxed base and then heated from underneath, the solder from the joints will run along the length of the wires, securing them. This should avoid excess solder flooding onto the base, which would discolour the

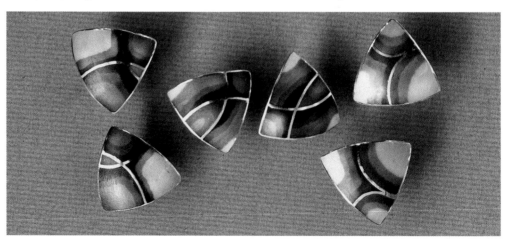

Earstuds in hardenable silver and cloisonné. 1986. Sarah Macrae.

Cloison wires.

enamels. It is surprising how little solder is needed to secure the wires. If any more needs to be added, the piece must be cleaned and refluxed. A very small piece of solder, the size of a pinhead, should be positioned vertically on the place that needs the extra fix, the edge of the cloisons given a thin, soft pencil line to inhibit the new solder from spreading onto the base and the piece heated from underneath.

Another method is to solder individual wires to the base, in which case it is important to fashion the cloisons so that they stand free, either by putting a curve in them or, if the design is geometric, bending them at an angle. It can be helpful to hold the wires in place with gum while the soldering is completed. One of the advantages of making the network first is that it is easier to ensure that the wires meet and flow into each other and you are

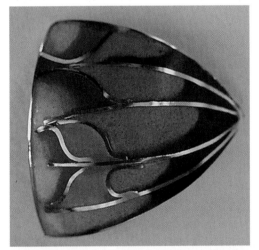

Silver brooches with cloisonné butterfly wings. 1985. Sarah Macrae.

Applying heat to the inside of a ring to solder wires.

not so likely to have gaps spoiling the final appearance of the enamelled piece.

If the wires are to decorate a curved side, such as a ring, bangle, or napkin ring, you can use the same method of making the network of wires, starting from a drawing. Once the wires are soldered together they can be gently curved over the shape of the piece which is to receive it or a triblet, bracelet mandrel or similar metal former. Obviously all the wires must touch the shank of the ring or the curve of any other piece. Secure the wires in place with twisted binding wire, coat with flux and direct the flame to the inside of the ring or bangle to draw the solder down onto the base to flow under the wires.

The inside of a small bowl can be dealt with in a similar way, except that the network of wires should be formed in a concave shape. If pure silver or a high-karat gold is used the wires can usually be manipulated by the fingers pressing the wires into the concave space, but if harder metal wire is used, it may be necessary to make a wooden former to fit the shape and gently press the wires down into the bowl. Titanium or steel sprung clips can be put in place round the edge of the bowl to hold the wires while the soldering takes place.

More complex and undulating shapes can be designed if hardenable silver is used. A piece of N-quality sheet can easily be shaped, as in this annealed state it is as soft as pure silver. Interesting forms can

Necklace (detail) in white and yellow gold with cloisonné. 1994. Jeanne Werge-Hartley.

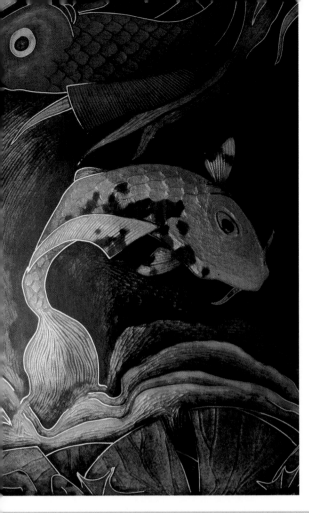

be domed, bent and repoussé worked, then irreversibly hardened in a kiln. Once the shape is hardened and rigid it can be used as a former over which a cloison network can be pressed to fit closely to the curve and held in place with binding wire. Remember to clean off the white layer (magnesium) that appears each time the silver is heated and that can be removed easily with a fine abrasive rubber. The soldering should be done as quickly as possible to stop the magnesium film from appearing between the wires and the silver base. After the wires are securely soldered in place, remove any traces of the white deposit before starting to lay in the enamels. Although preparing this metal seems a little tedious to begin with, the advantages soon outweigh the extra work: there is no firestain, the enamel colour is true and the shapes will not warp or collapse in the kiln (*see* Chapter 3).

Kingfisher Vase (detail), showing gold wire used over silver cloisonné. 1996. Fred Rich.

Butterfly Salt. Fred Rich.

SARAH MACRAE

Penannular pins are a speciality of Sarah's jewellery, and her combination of materials is often dramatic and unusual. She makes integral fastenings a feature of her work, as in brooch fastenings and necklaces. Many of her pieces are reversible, often enamelled on one side with inlaid ebony on the other.

Sarah started enamelling in the workshop of her mother, Jeanne Werge-Hartley, as a young girl and developed her ideas and techniques on a combined Wood, Metals,

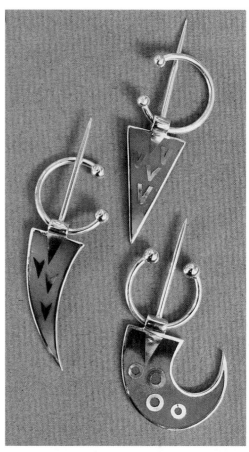

Penannular brooches with matching ring, all in silver and shaded enamel. 1987.
Sarah Macrae.

Paper knives in pure silver and enamel. 1991. Sarah Macrae.

Reversible earrings in ebony and enamel. 1994. Sarah Macrae.

FOLLOWING PAGE: Penannular brooch in silver and cloisonné. 1990. Sarah Macrae.

Ceramics and Plastics degree course at Brighton Polytechnic. There was no enamelling tuition at the college but with her background knowledge she was able to incorporate enamelling in the jewellery for her final show. She was chosen to exhibit at the Arnolfini Gallery as one of the promising students in Britain of that year and was also awarded a distinction licentiateship of the Society of Designer Craftsmen. Sarah has been a member of the Designer Jewellers Group since 1980 and has exhibited annually with the group in London and other national venues.

Since leaving college Sarah has taught part time at Sir John Cass College, Portsmouth College of Art and LSU College, Southampton, and is currently teaching short courses in jewellery at West Dean College, Sussex. At the same time Sarah has worked to private commissions and for exhibitions. She has always used hardenable silver with great success and also incorporates fine silver on occasion. She uses enamels with a subtle blending of colours which often range from deep greys through to pale aquamarines and off-white. The colours are frequently interrupted by applied cloisonné lines or shapes such as circles and arrowheads; she also uses sheets saw-pierced with patterns in contrast to fine wire detail. Her ideas and inspiration often emanate from the muted colours of bird feathers and butterfly markings.

Many of her penannulars, hairpins and rings are constructed with hidden hinges to allow flexibility, not only in movement when worn as earrings, but also to enable the pieces to be enamelled as separate units before being joined to the more solid part of the design.

The high quality of her drawing skills is the result of continuous mark making from an early age and translates into metal with an elegance of shape and line. This combines with her engineering skills to produce work that is thoughtfully designed and made to the highest standards of finish.

6 PLIQUE A JOUR

DEFINITION AND HISTORY

Plique à jour is possibly the most exacting of all the enamelling techniques, but is also one of the most beautiful aspects of the applied arts. Pieces of this enamel work resemble miniature stained glass windows, as the transparent enamel is held in small cloisons which are open at the back to allow the light to pass through. To get the most out of the colour and brilliance of plique à jour, the designer must consider where the piece will be seen; for example, pendant earrings and hair ornaments are ideal places to show how exquisite this method can be. Cups and bowls also present wonderful opportunities for the enameller to create three-dimensional objects.

An exhibition at Goldsmiths' Hall in May 1987 gave Britain an opportunity to view and admire the enamels of René Lalique (1860–1945). One could only marvel at the brilliance of his jewellery, which in many cases incorporated intricate areas of plique à jour. Possibly the most famous of his pieces is his enormous dragonfly corsage ornament, which measures 27×26.5cm and has the most exquisite gold hinged wings of iridescent shaded blue/green plique à jour enamel, with the wing markings in foiled blue/green enamel within pools of diamonds and moonstones.

TECHNIQUES

There are several plique à jour techniques, all of which require patience, dedication and the ability to accept failure and start again.

Preparing the Metal

Possibly the method which presents the fewest problems is one that involves saw piercing or photo-etching a pattern of small, rounded shapes in a piece of sheet silver, approximately 16 gauge. These cells should not be larger than about 6×20mm.

Butterfly plique à jour bowl, with gold cloisonné and silver and gold base. 1999. Alexandra Raphael.

Long, thin shapes and sharp corners should be avoided, as these will give rise to stress in the enamel and lead to crazing.

The design can be transferred to the metal in a number of ways before saw piercing. One method is to trace the design onto self-adhesive paper and attach it to the metal. Drill holes at the edge of each cell, then pass the saw blade through a hole and saw the cell out. Saw out the other cells in the same way. If the blade is held at a slight angle the cells will be a little smaller at the back, which will give the enamel a better hold. The finer the saw blade (5/0 to 8/0) the less there is to true up after sawing. The piece of metal must then be cleaned and degreased.

ABOVE: Dragonfly brooch in silver and plique à jour. 2001. Hali Baykov.

LEFT: Silver plique à jour goblet with a 'lace' design. 1993. Alexandra Raphael.

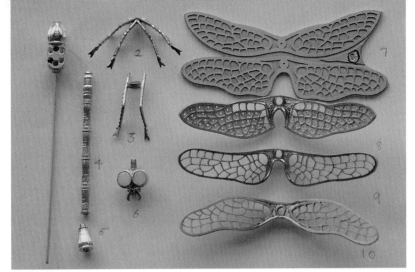

Preparing the Enamels

For plique à jour there seem to be two schools of thought concerning the grinding of the enamels. One is that the enamel should not be ground as fine as for backed pieces and that the grains should resemble granulated sugar in texture (60 mesh or even coarser). Alternatively, as Erica Speel writes in her *Dictionary of Enamelling*, the enamel should be ground to a paste of 80 mesh or finer. It may be that the size of the cell is the deciding factor, so keeping a record of experiences may enable you to make a personal decision. In any case, it is imperative to wash the enamels very carefully, as any impurities will impair the transparency and colour; there should be no residue or silt left in the water when you have finished rinsing. Although pre-ground contemporary enamels are acceptable as long as they are washed in distilled water until all the impurities are eliminated, it is infinitely preferable to use lump enamels and grind fresh amounts prior to use. It is also important to choose your colours with care, bearing in mind that the darker ones allow less light through. The washed enamels can be kept clean by transferring them to individual small plastic containers, covering the enamel with a little pure water and placing a lid, plastic sheet or cling film over the container to keep out the specks of dust that are in the air.

Backing

When the clean silver piece is ready to be filled with enamel it should be placed on a

TOP: Photo-etched parts and connecting units for dragonfly brooch.

MIDDLE: Butterfly brooch, photo-etched and assembled before enamelling.

BOTTOM: Butterfly brooch in silver and plique à jour. 2001. Hali Baykov.

backing to which it will not adhere permanently. There are several backings you can use, each of which has its own peculiarities.

• **Mica** The cheapest and most used material. Split the mica into thin pieces to avoid blistering and, if it is new, give it a quick firing to eliminate any blisters. Mica that has already been used but is clean is the best choice.
• **Copper foil** Enamel adheres to copper, so the copper has to be removed after firing by immersing it in nitric acid. The front of the piece should be protected by wax or a similar stop-out.
• **Gold foil** The enamel will fuse to the gold, which then has to be filed off or etched away by dabbing or soaking in a tepid solution of Aqua Regis. At today's gold prices this is a waste of precious metal.
• **Titanium** The metal needs to be cleaned with rough emery paper before reusing to remove any oxide, but in recent experiments both silver and enamel have come away cleanly from the backing. An added advantage of using titanium is that it can support curved pieces. Other refractory metals such as niobium and tantalum may be used as long as the metal is not already anodized or oxidized. Experiments with these have been encouraging.
• **Platinum** This is the best backing to use if really good results are a priority. It peels off after the final firing, leaving a clean and glossy surface. It is expensive initially but, as it can be used over and over again as long as it is well looked after, it is certainly worth the investment (*see* Chapter 3).

Packing the Cells

There are a number of ways to ensure that the piece of silver to be enamelled is not only kept in place on the backing (mica or metal) but also placed so that the wet enamel does not seep underneath. Bent steel pins or titanium clips can be used and this is made easier when using Kaowool Ceramic Fibre. However, if the silver is very flat, it is possible to brush a little gum tragacanth or Klyrfyre on to the backing, sit the silver on top and leave it to dry. On small pieces this is often sufficient to hold it in place while the cells are filled. Before starting to pack the washed enamels, a touch of gum tragacanth or Klyrfyre round the edge of the cell will help the enamel to adhere to the silver. In larger areas it is also possible to add a little of the gum solution to the wet enamel, or to drop a little into the enamel during the packing process as this will help the enamel to stay in the space but will disappear during the firing.

With a very fine sable paintbrush or quill carefully lay the wet enamel into each cell, using a needle to push it firmly into the edges if necessary, then gently press down with a small spatula and a piece of tissue (or blotting paper) to eliminate any air bubbles. More enamel can be piled in the centre of the cell, as it will sink during the firing. Once all the cells are filled, the piece should be covered to keep it clean and left to dry by the kiln. When it is dry, gently tap the edge of the piece, which will level the enamel and eliminate any pockets of air.

Firing

Fire in a hot kiln. Depending on the metal, silver or gold, the temperature should be between 900°C (1652°F) and 1000°C (1832°F). When the kiln is at the correct temperature the piece should be fired high and fast. If the temperature is too low the enamel will be underfired and will collect in the middle of the cell instead of spreading up the cell walls to form the flat pool of colour required. When the enamel is bright red and has become smooth the piece should be withdrawn from the kiln and allowed to cool slowly.

When the enamel is cold it may need to be cleaned briefly in dilute sulphuric acid if using standard silver or certain karat golds. Then carefully stone down the front surface with carborundum stone or a fine wet and dry emery stick. It is important to do this with great care as the enamel at this stage is very fragile. A pad of folded paper towel over a block of wood will serve as a cushion to support the piece while working. Also at this stage any defects can be eliminated by using a dentist's burr held in a pin vice to gently take out any blemish or to widen a bubble under the surface for refilling.

Before any further refilling it is important that the piece is well washed with warm soapy water containing a little ammonia and flushed under running water. Then it can be repositioned on the mica, pegged or glued, refilled and refired; if necessary, this process can be repeated until the enamel is level, free of pinholes and ready for the final procedure. In a simple piece two preliminary firings are often sufficient. After you have stoned the reverse side, removed any remaining flecks of mica and give the piece a short clean in dilute sulphuric acid, wash the piece thoroughly again, possibly using a glass brush or, if possible, giving it a few minutes in an ultrasonic cleaner.

Now the piece is ready for the final flash firing that will produce the beautiful, pure, glowing colours. To achieve this the piece is suspended on an iron wire support, or balanced on a trivet so that only the metal surround is touching the support. Fire the enamel high and very fast. When the piece has cooled it should be placed in dilute sulphuric acid once more for a very short time to clean the metal, then washed under running water and dried in a soft paper towel.

Polishing

The silver can be given a matt surface or a high polish depending on what finish is required, and may be machine or hand polished. During the polishing process the enamel must be supported on a wood surface slightly larger than the enamel so that it is not scratched or stressed. If standard silver has been used all firestain should be removed – before attempting to polish – by

using Water of Ayr stone or Garriflex abrasive. A matt finish is produced by rubbing with one or more of the following compounds: a fibreglass brush, pumice powder, Garriflex abrasive or a steel brush on the flexi-drive. If a polished finish is required the silver should be either burnished or machine polished with great care.

PLIQUE À JOUR USING CLOISONNÉ WIRES

Another method of producing plique à jour is by soldering cloisonné wires, which can be held within a framework of thicker wire to strengthen them while being part of the design. Although enamelling solder flows at a higher temperature than most enamels it is sensible to use as little as possible; the piece can be designed with this in mind to reduce the soldering points needed. For example, using one length of wire it is possible to make a pattern that will need very few soldered contact points.

Making the Cloisonné Wire

Fine silver or gold is preferable for making the wire, the size of which is determined by the design. Generally the wire is 0.2–0.3mm thick and 1.5–1.8mm deep (rolling round 0.4mm wire can achieve this). Perimeter wires can be thicker, from 1.27mm to 2.03mm, depending on the scale of the piece. However, an experienced and innovative designer will vary the sizes to achieve more interesting and exciting linear patterns. Some enamellers use a concave wire made by pulling a rectangular wire through a round drawplate using a hole which is slightly smaller in diameter than the depth of the rectangular wire. The U-shaped wire holds the enamel very well, but you may find connecting the wires to each other to form the design a little tricky. The wires must be annealed to form the shapes and, because the metal is soft and easily damaged, it is advisable to manipulate the wires with index finger and

Soldering plique à jour wires.

thumb as much as possible, rather than with tools.

An Introductory Piece

Take a length of annealed rectangular wire approximately 16mm long and form it into an abstract pattern of small shapes so that the wire comes back on itself to close the cell each time. The areas must be small, sharp points must be avoided (also long thin shapes at this stage) and the piece needs to be kept flat. Make sure the wires are touching at the edges then place the piece on the soldering block. Because this piece will be very delicate, place it on a used piece of thin mica and put this on a mesh stand, which will enable the flame to be directed underneath. Put very small paillons of enamelling solder (rolled thin and cut into pinhead-sized pieces) on the outside of the wires with a flux. Allow the flux to dry and then apply a soft flame under the wires until the solder flows. Clean in pickle. This a good method for soldering all wirework, varying the types of heat depending on the size of the piece; it is surprising how little heat is required if this procedure is followed.

Preparation of the Enamels
Once again the grinding and washing of the enamels should be done immediately prior to packing and, although this makes it slightly more difficult to pack the enamel into the cells, the grains should be larger than in other methods (about 60 mesh) for greater clarity of colour.

Packing and Firing
Place the piece on the chosen backing and hold it in place with a little gum solution and bent pins. The sides of the cells may be coated with a little gum, but as you gain experience you may find this is not always necessary. Wet pack the cells with a very fine sable paint brush, pushing well to the edges, but do not overfill as it is preferable to have two or three thin layers rather than one thick one. Remove excess water with blotting paper or tissue and leave the covered piece by the kiln to dry. The first firing should leave the surface of the enamel looking like granulated sugar. Cool, refill, and fire again until the enamel is level with the wires and has a glassy finish. At this point check for air bubbles and impurities and, if necessary, remove them with dental burrs, clean thoroughly, refill and refire. It may be possible at this stage to remove the mica backing, stone the back and flash fire with the piece supported on a trivet.

WORKING FROM A CONSIDERED DESIGN

An advanced piece of plique à jour, which may have a complex arrangement of wires and cells, needs to have the design drawn clearly on paper or card and covered in some form of transparent plastic covering. The individual wires can be shaped over the design and even tacked down with a little gum to keep them in place until the cell shapes are completed and ready to be soldered. Curved wires stand up easily on their own but, if straighter

Using one length of wire.

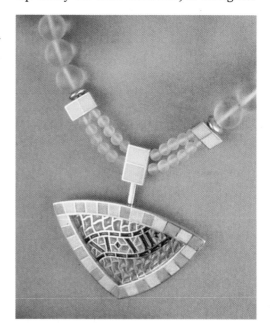

Necklace in silver, plique à jour and champlevé with frosted glass beads. 1992. Phil Barnes.

lines are needed, it is easier to anchor one end by soldering it in place as a curve and then straighten it. The ends of the wires must be trued to fit so they have very close contact with the wire to which they are going to be soldered. This is to ensure that as little solder as possible is used to make the join.

Soldering

The method described previously can be used here though obviously it is not always necessary, or even possible, to solder the whole piece in one go. It is important to make the paillons of enamelling solder as small as possible and to heat the wires from underneath with a gentle flame. When all the wires are soldered, clean the piece in acid to remove the residue of flux.

Preparation

After grinding and washing the selected colours it is sensible to test them on a piece of mica to ensure that they are compatible and will fire at the same temperature. These samples can be mounted for future reference – an experienced enameller will have not only a personal collection of samples, but be very knowledgeable about the range of enamels used. If you are using a variety of colours it is helpful to number the dishes so that you can refer back to the design sheet for subsequent firings and future repeat pieces.

Packing and Firing

Although mica is perfectly acceptable to use as a backing, for a larger and more complex piece, platinum foil or a piece of refractory metal will give a much better result. Secure the wire structure to the backing by anchoring with bent pins, which will ensure that there is no seepage of the enamel under the wires, and place the mica and piece on a trivet of mesh before filling. For platinum, a clean piece of thin fire brick must be used to prevent damage and contamination to the platinum.

The method for laying in the wet enamel and firing is the same as already described except that with a more complex piece more time and concentration is needed. Three firings are normal, plus a final flash firing once it is certain that there are no air bubbles or impurities to impair the clarity.

Finishing

There are two ways to finish the piece, and you will have to decide which to use before packing the enamel into the cloisons. The first is to fill and fire to the level of the wires, then stone down to expose the wires, wash thoroughly with hot soapy water, then clean water and then flash fire. The other way is to pack and fire so that the enamel is concave in the centre of the cells. This method allows more light through and is particularly interesting with darker, richer colours. It can also be achieved by carefully carving out the centre with diamond tipped drills in a flexi-drive before flash firing.

Cleaning and Polishing

After each firing clean the piece in dilute sulphuric acid, as this makes it easier to see the wires and remove any enamel that has spilt on to them. Various tools are useful for cleaning the wires (*see* Chapter 3) and hand polishing is certainly the easiest method for plique à jour, as long as the piece is always well supported. This way is much more controllable and allows you to polish the wires as required.

PLIQUE A JOUR WITHOUT SOLDERING

An alternative way of making the cells is to embed the wires into a thin layer of clear enamel flux on a backing of copper foil. One of the great advantages of this particular method is that it is possible to produce curved objects by shaping the copper backing first. After firing, the copper can be etched away with nitric acid, leaving the thin layer of transparent enamel and the cloisons. These cells should be filled and fired as with other methods. Finally, the clear flux needs to be removed, either by stoning, or very carefully with dental burrs in a flexi-drive, and the piece flash-fired.

Cups and Bowls

A second method of making a curved or undulating piece of plique à jour is to use a former or caisson which can be enamelled against, but which will release the enamel cleanly after being fired. A former can be made from a shaped piece of titanium, or a piece of stainless steel covered in small pieces of mica (or titanium or platinum foil) secured in place with gum tragacanth. The annealed cloisonné network is pressed over or into the caisson and held in place with cotter pins or binding wire secured tightly by threading it over notches filed on the edge of the caisson and wrapping it round the whole piece (do not allow the binding wire to touch the enamel). The piece is then packed, dried and fired. If any further firings are required the mica or foil must be replaced, and if a titanium caisson has been used it should be cleaned with coarse emery paper to remove the oxide.

OTHER METHODS AND USEFUL IDEAS

Plique à Jour without Backing

There is an interesting method of filling larger cells without using a backing, relying on water tension alone to hold the enamel in place. Suspend the piece to be enamelled horizontally on a well-made and stable iron wire frame. Using a fine paint brush apply a thin layer of wet enamel round the edge of each cell. Fire the piece to 'granulated sugar' stage, being careful not to overfire, which would allow the enamel to pull away from the edges. Repeat until the whole cell is covered in a cobwebby surface. At this stage add several thin layers of wet enamel,

taking each one to the crystalline stage and repeating until the enamel is flush with the wires. Stone the piece and hand polish both sides with carborundum sticks and graduated wet and dry papers until the enamel is clear of flaws. Wash it several times to be sure that all the dirt is removed and then flash fire it. Skill and patience is required for this process!

Protecting Surrounding Metal

If the area of plique à jour is held within a framework, or is part of a bigger piece of jewellery, protect the areas of surrounding metal (possibly already cleaned and polished) from stray grains of enamel by applying a thin coat of powdered rouge and methylated spirit, taking care not to contaminate the enamel.

Plique à jour ring. Silver, 24K and enamel. Jeanne Werge-Hartley 2005.

ALEXANDRA RAPHAEL

Alexandra Raphael is internationally known and respected for her enamelling and especially for her delicate plique à jour bowls. She will readily tell you that over the last twenty years the bowls have provided her with an ongoing learning experience. Each bowl is completely different from the previous one and each one overcomes the difficulties and problems encountered while making the one before. This progressive

development of Alexandra's work is as fascinating as her bowls are beautiful, and any flaws in her early pieces only emphasize how far she has come in her techniques to master this complex and difficult art form.

Alexandra was born in the USA, the daughter of two artists, so, as she explains, it was inevitable that she became interested in the arts herself. Originally she had contemplated a career in biology, and maybe this is where her interest in the flora and fauna which decorate so many of her pieces began. Alexandra attended the University of Iowa for two years studying photography and film

Frog and tadpoles bowl in silver plique à jour with a silver cloisonné-enamelled base. 1998. Alexandra Raphael.

Necklace enamelled in rare-earth pink over fine silver enamelled beads with blue topaz beads. 1994. Alexandra Raphael.

making, then went to live in Ireland with her painter husband. She says that one of the advantages of this period was having the time to develop her individuality of design while working full time in enamelling, but the downside was being so isolated and not being able to find any technical help.

In 1981 she moved to London and started making cloisonné enamelled beads, which she enjoyed as it gave her the opportunity to enamel different designs on each side. In 1988 she introduced a new element to her pieces by including secret messages, and says that she was intrigued by the thought of people spending time holding these pieces and discovering her hidden words.

Alexandra still makes beads and achieves the most lovely colours, especially exquisite pinks and succulent reds. Her beads are raised or domed in fine silver and made in two halves joined with a standard silver

rim to cover the solder seam. The cloisons are curved and fitted to the shape of the bead, where they are held in place with Klyrfyre while she lays in the enamels and fires them.

Alexandra was inspired to attempt the plique à jour or 'window of day' method of enamelling after finding a Japanese bowl in an antique shop. She says she spent two years just looking at it and trying to work out how it had been made, as at that time, around 1978, no one else she knew of was making such items. She started in a simple way by forming the letters of her name in cloisonné wires, but put the letters in reverse and, in order to read her name, was obliged to make her first piece of plique à jour.

In 1980 she progressed to her first bowl in plique à jour, which she completed three years later. This was a very simple daisy pattern carried out in just four colours. Although inevitably there were problems Alexandra felt that the bowl was a beginning and was sufficiently encouraged to continue and develop her ideas and techniques.

One of Alexandra's bowls was featured on the 1998 Channel 4 programme *Collectors' Lot*, where the making from start to finish was filmed over a two-month period. Alexandra works over a copper form which she has spun for her and, in this particular bowl, called Frog and Tadpoles with Fish, 9.5m of fine silver cloisonné wire was used to curve and fashion the shapes of the pond creatures to fit over the surface of the copper. This took four days. Then she gently fired the wires in a kiln to attach them to the copper bowl former with flux.

After grinding and washing the enamels, they were applied between the wires and given their first firing at 800°C (1472°F). Subsequent layers of enamel were inlaid and fired until they reached the level of the wires. The surface of the enamel was then stoned with diamond impregnated paper to ensure a flat, smooth finish. A

Butterfly bowl (detail). Alexandra Raphael.

final hot and fast firing restored the shine on the enamel and the silver wires were given a final clean and polish with pumice, soap and water. Alexandra then removed the copper form with a weak solution of nitric acid, protecting the silver wires by masking them with wax. This lengthy process eventually revealed the transparency and luminosity of the plique à jour. Many of Alexandra's bowls need twenty to thirty firings.

Alexandra has won many prizes for her bowls over the past few years at the Goldsmiths' Craft Council Awards, Goldsmiths' Hall in London and the plique à jour prize in the Palm Beach Enamel Guild Award 1991. Her work, both jewellery and bowls, is included in permanent collections in Limoges, Geneva, and Moscow. Together with a group of fellow artists, Alexandra recently opened a gallery dedicated to contemporary glass enamelling called Studio Fusion which is located in the Oxo Tower Wharf, London. The gallery shows the work of many of today's enamellers and the exciting work of new graduates.

Necklace in silver and champlevé. Hali Baykov.

K. HALI BAYKOV

Hali's plique à jour dragonflies and butter-flies have won her many awards between 1987 and 2001 in the Goldsmiths' Craft Council Competition. She also won a Maureen Carswell Award in 2000, the Fred Barnes Memorial Award in 2001 and was made Enameller Elect of the 2001 conference of the Guild of Enamellers.

Hali was born in Prague, Czechoslovakia, of Ukrainian parents, came to live in England in 1946 and trained at St Martin's School of Art as a graphic designer. She attended a jewellery class at Sir John Cass School of Art and later became a part-time day student, eventually specializing in designer jewellery with an enamelling emphasis. Hali was one of the early members of the British Society of Enamellers and has shown her work in many of the Society's exhibitions in London, Cambridge and in Germany. She has also exhibited in Ohio, Madrid, and in an international exhibition in Japan.

Not all of Hali's work is plique à jour, and necklaces with enamelled flowers and leaves are carried out in champlevé. One particularly fine necklace is of two passion flowers, each about 6cm across, and a leaf curving over a neckband, reaffirming Hali's affinity with natural forms. Her dragonfly brooch shows how all the individual parts of the dragonfly are delicately engineered and illustrate the expertise of her craftsmanship. Each piece is assembled with pins and screws and often set with stones once the wings and bodies have been enamelled. The wings are photo-etched and the cells for the plique à jour enamel sawn out leaving an intricate tracery of holes. The enamelled wings are secured by gem-set screws and pegged into the body, which has been turned on a lathe, engraved and enamelled. Hali's keen interest and observation is evident in her detailing of these beautiful insects. Hali says:

To me jewellery should be a work of art and not just an adornment. When I make a piece of jewellery I hope it will be displayed when it is not being worn, and to achieve this I try to make it three-dimensional, with plenty of movement, either in shape or construction. I use transparent enamels on engraved, textured or carved metal to give extra depth to the work.

ANN SMITH

In 1987 Ann Smith and her husband opened a small jewellery gallery called Peacock House in the lovely town of Chipping Camden, where, in 1902, C.R. Ashbee moved the Guild of Handicrafts and opened his workshops.

Ann originally practised as a dentist but, disenchanted with this work, she took an enamelling summer-school course at West Dean College. However, it took a visit to the Hull Grundy Collection at the British Museum finally to decide her career change, as one particular piece, a gold cloisonné enamelled locket by Alexis Falize, encouraged her to enrol at Sir

Brooch in 18K yellow gold, opal and plique à jour. Ann Smith.

Brooch in 18K yellow gold, aquamarine and plique à jour. Ann Smith.

John Cass College, where she spent four years learning to make fine jewellery.

Currently all Ann's pieces are made in 18K gold, some of them plique à jour enamelled. In the past she has made larger items, such as a silver ordination chalice, the base of which is engraved basse taille transparent green enamel to complement the Sutherland tapestry in Coventry Cathedral. Other large pieces include a cloisonné silver cruet set and a seven-day chiming clock.

Ann admits that the challenging techniques of enamelling on metal have put enchantment back into her life and she hopes that some of this has passed to her patrons, who have made it possible for her to continue.

7 OTHER TECHNIQUES

PAINTED OR LIMOGES ENAMEL

This form of painted enamelling calls for considerably more appreciation of drawing, composition and colour than do other techniques. Painted enamels are used on many kinds of article, from large vessels to miniatures set in jewellery. They are at their most beautiful in the decorative panels and miniatures produced in France during the eighteenth and nineteenth centuries. This form of enamelling uses finely ground enamel colours mixed with oil and painted on to a base. The base is enamelled with an opaque or transparent ground and may be of silver or gold, although copper is sometimes used. In the fifteenth century Limoges' jewellers became highly skilled at painted enamel work and it was in this period that the French craftsmen established that the metal divisions between enamels were not essential and started to paint with enamel directly on to the metal.

The procedure is complicated if realistic forms are to be interpreted, as the drawing and rendering of these forms needs an absolute knowledge of the relative hardness and firing temperatures of all the colours being used, so that the colours painted first do not spoil in the kiln heat required for the later colours. The first firings are high and the subsequent colours are of a progressively lower firing temperature.

Lucy with Teasel in painted enamel. 1996. Gillie Hoyte Byrom.

Method

Enamels used for painting are similar to those used for other enamelling techniques but they are ground to a much finer consistency and mixed with various essential oils (*see* Chapter 2). There are three stages in building up a painting and it usually takes between eight or nine firings in total. The first is the base or grounding, the second is the application of the design or portrait and the third is a final layer of protective flux. The actual metal base of the piece can be silver, gold or copper and the shape can be flat or domed slightly, and it is always counter-enamelled.

The enamels are supplied in powder form in airtight containers and, when not in use, they should be kept airtight, dry and free from dust. To prepare the enamels put out only sufficient for the day's use onto a piece of glass, porcelain or agate.

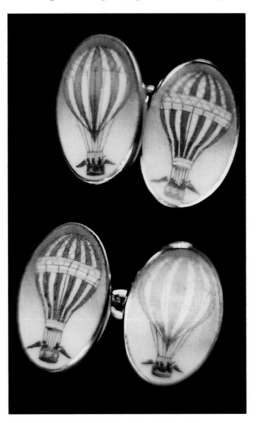

Cufflinks in 18K gold (made by Brixton & Gill) and painted enamel. Dayna White.

Using a steel palette knife add a very small quantity of oil and, with a brisk circular motion, triturate the two together, by applying gentle pressure with the end of a knife. From time to time apply greater pressure to release the knife from the colour; gather the colour into a small heap and continue mixing as before until the blending of the colour and oil is complete. This usually takes about two minutes. Keep each colour on a separate palette and covered until all the colours are mixed. It is very important that the colours are kept scrupulously clean and covered at all times except when in use.

Enamel painting is usually carried out on opaque white, cream, pale pastel-coloured or opal white backgrounds, though it is possible to use black or transparent dark blue. Even though the ground enamel which is applied first is covered by subsequent layers it is essential that it is prepared and applied with great care, as impurities and air pockets are likely to rise to the surface during late firings. Three thin fired layers of the ground enamel are needed to give a good base to work on. After the third firing the piece should be stoned flat, washed and refired.

The design or outline can be drawn on the fired ground using a graphite pencil or a mapping nib with enamel paint; in both cases the lines will fade in the later firings. The image is built up in layers and firings, the number of which depends on the complexity of the design. Each successive stage of the painting should be carefully thought out beforehand to try to keep the number of firings to a minimum and so reduce the risk of failure. Apply each thin coat with a very fine sable brush. Put the enamel on in small touches close together and smooth it out with a fine brush with light cross strokes.

Drying the enamel piece before placing it in the kiln is vital to allow the oils mixed with the enamels to evaporate before firing, and this should be done as soon as

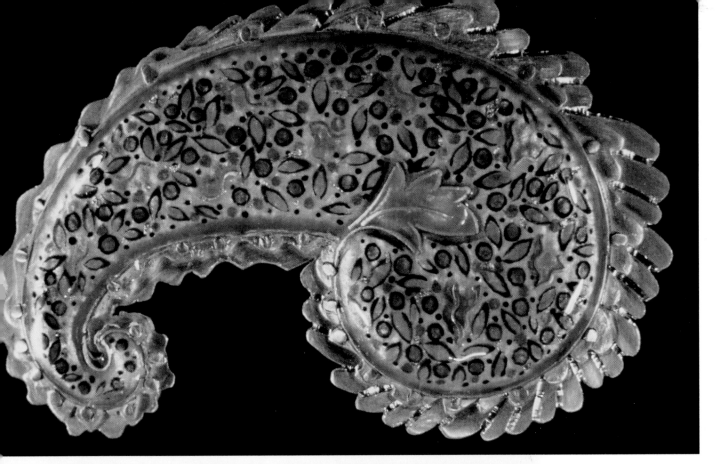

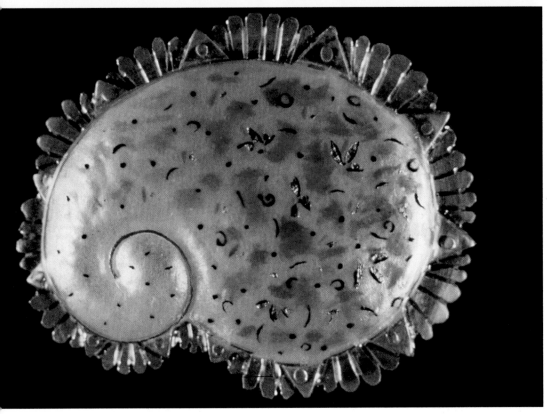

Painted enamel plaque. Dayna White.

possible after applying the enamels. The piece should be offered up to the kiln slowly to avoid heating it too quickly, but once inside the kiln the firing time is usually only ten to thirty seconds; you must take great care not to overfire, as this dulls the colours. Each layer is fired between 750°C (1382°F) and 850°C (1562°F). When the colours begin to gloss over they will have fused to the ground sufficiently for the next layer to be applied. The first layer is always the pale background colours, the second layer builds up the picture and the fine detail of the foreground,

while the finishing touches are applied in the third layer.

Finally, two to three thin layers of flux are added to give a protective covering, which also helps to soften down the edges of the painting. The flux must be prepared as carefully as the painting enamels, applied each time in a very thin coat and fired. After the final layer has been fired the whole surface is stoned, washed and refired to give a smooth and glossy surface. The piece can now be polished, plated or electroformed. It takes time and experience to discover which enamels are suitable for

particular requirements and to understand the reactions of different colours. Gold and silver metal lustres can be applied during a final dull red firing. Once the piece is cool the areas can be burnished.

GRISAILLE

Grisaille is a method of surface painting enamel in a gradation of whites and greys on a dark blue or black background. It is usually made on a counter-enamelled copper plaque although precious metals may be used. The monochrome picture is achieved by layers of opaque white enamel, which are first used very thinly to allow the background to show through to give a delicate and translucent effect. Subsequently the image is built up in layers of white enamel of varying thickness, firing between each application. The final layers are dense and often give a slight relief and an overall three-dimensional effect. The American artist enameller, Bill Helwig, applies grisaille techniques to his work. He breaks many of the traditional rules and achieves stunningly beautiful results.

Brooches in silver and painted enamel (autumn leaves). 1999. Ruth Ball.

An early mention of grisaille was made in 1420 in an inventory of gold and jewellery belonging to Philip the Good, Duke of Burgundy, and the artists of the Netherlandish School were known to have used the technique and applied it to goblets and beakers in borders decorated with animals. The Limoges School perfected the art of grisaille, and the development of the process was attributed to the Penicauld workshops in about 1520.

As in other forms of painted enamels, such as ronde bosse, the grisaille enamels of the sixteenth century became more complex and contained figurative allegorical scenes. Borders and surrounds of larger pieces were decorated with scrolls and grotesques and other ornamentation. The figures were beautifully drawn and modelled in bas relief, and the thick layering of the enamel paint gave the pictures a feeling of perspective. When the Limoges School revivalists in the nineteenth century started to copy these enamels, it is interesting to note that they required twelve to twenty-five stages of firing. Traditionally grisaille is painted in tones of white, sometimes outlined with gold, which is prepared as a liquid and used for halos and other decoration. Occasionally the monotones were overlaid with translucent enamel, usually to give a minimal flesh tone to the faces and limbs of the figures.

Method

The base may be made of copper or precious metal onto which a thin ground of dark blue or black high-firing enamel is fused, and fired simultaneously with a counter-enamel. Then add two separately fired layers of the blue or black enamel, stone the surface until smooth, wash thoroughly and refire. Prepare the white enamel with medium and use a sable brush to apply the design. Well-thinned enamel will fade into the background while thicker enamel will remain as well-defined shapes and lines. Begin by painting the shadows and shaded areas, gradually building up the design, and finish with the thickest enamel to form the highlights. Do not put the piece in acid between firings but stone the metal edge to stop the oxides contaminating the enamel. Blot each application of paste dry, warm and fire at 785°C (1450°F). Take the piece out of the kiln as soon as the enamel begins to glaze, as overfiring will allow the white to start spreading. To unify the final surface an even, thin layer of clear enamel or flux can be applied over the whole surface and the piece refired.

RONDE BOSSE

The French art form of émail en ronde bosse, developed in the fourteenth century, is the enamelling of figures and forms that are sculpted in low relief or totally in the round. The metal is usually gold, although silver and copper have also been used. The metal can be entirely covered in enamel or only partly, and both opaque and translucent enamels can be used. Very expensive and ornate enamelled articles were made in the fifteenth and early sixteenth centuries incorporating miniature sculptures of animals and mythical creatures. Often these secular pieces, such as large table salts and fountains, were not only embellished with the enamelled figures and other decorative elements but also encrusted with pearls and gemstones.

In the sixteenth century the technique of enamelling in the round was used for the encapsulation of wealth in jewellery, and large pendants and brooches were made with innovative designs surrounding an asymmetrical pearl or stone. The goldsmith was allowed to create fantasy, and often produced allegorical masterpieces in high-relief chased gold and enamel. An example is the jewelled insignia worn by a Knight of the Garter that incorporates the figures of St George and the Dragon in enamelled bas relief. The Renaissance period produced many splendid examples across Europe as gold-smiths like Benvenuto Cellini vied with each other to make articles of excellence and virtuosity. There are collections of Renaissance ronde bosse pieces in the British Museum, the jewellery gallery in the Victoria and Albert Museum and many other major museums.

The nineteenth century brought a re-vival in interest in this technique by jew-ellery craftsmen in Paris and many fakes of Renaissance enamels were made. To-day the tradition of using this form of en-amelling has continued in insignia work and the Garter jewels. A contemporary use of the technique is for badges by embossing and dye stamping, while many studio pieces are made by casting units for necklaces and other pieces of jewellery and enamelling them with transparent colours. The goldsmith's craftsmanship needs to be of the highest calibre for the chasing and carving of the reliefs, and the applied enamel has to be thin enough to follow every small contour of the figures.

Method

Traditionally, three-dimensional designs are made by chasing or repoussé, working into thin gold sheet or foil. The joining of the two halves by soldering has to with-stand the enamelling temperatures and, as normal with a hollow form, a small air hole must be left to allow air to escape during soldering and enamelling. This hole can be stoppered with a plug of wax or a tight-fitting silver wire while the piece is pickled. The hole can also be used to apply counter-enamel to the inside; and often very thin metal bas relief pieces are filled with plas-ter of Paris, which is invisible once the piece is mounted.

Small articles can sometimes be enam-elled and completed in one firing but it is usual to need two or more. The first firing should be a counter-enamelling slurry, which is swilled around the inside filling all the crevices and spaces. Lay the enamel onto the outside as a wet paste as thinly and as evenly as possible, taking care that it does not overfill in the hollows and spoil the transparency. Opaque white was used in the Renaissance period for the faces and limbs of the figures and also to highlight detail and raised decoration which contrasted with the gold background. Translucent enamels, such as blues, greens and occasionally reds, were applied to other areas.

It is important to make sure that the enamel is flat and even before drying com-pletely – excess moisture can be taken off with a soft tissue or linen pad. On large areas that are to be totally covered in enamel the piece can be brushed over or sprayed with a thin coating of gum and dry enamel powder sifted onto it. Dry the piece completely and slowly in front of the kiln on a stable support that is easy to put into the kiln. The first firing should only fuse to the 'orange peel' or dimpled sur-face stage; then remove the piece from the kiln and cool slowly. Any area where the enamel appears to be too thick can be stoned down, washed carefully and refired until the piece is satisfactory. Now the areas of bare metal can be polished in the normal way using all the stages of hand polishing to reduce the time needed on the polishing machine.

EMAIL EN RESILLE SUR VERRE

This is a little-known enamelling tech-nique that was practised by highly skilled French craftsmen in the seventeenth cen-tury, but which only lasted for about two decades. The technique involved engrav-ing lines into glass, which was usually dark blue or viridian, in a low intaglio. These engraved hollows were lined with ex-tremely thin gold foil and filled with wet enamel. The enamel had to be able to fuse at a low enough temperature not to affect the glass. The overall effect was extremely delicate and subtle.

PATE DE VERRE

This technique, in which a one-off cast in glass is produced from a clay mould, was developed in the nineteenth century and revived in the 1970s by Diana Hobson. A clay mould, such as a vase, is made and the interior is packed with grains of glass in a similar way to enamelling. The piece is fired for a long time as in ceramics, the mould is taken away and the pâte de verre product is revealed. This is a very difficult technique to master, and Diana has taken this old art form and, by incorporating found material such as hair and feathers, has extended and developed it.

RUTH BALL

During the 1990s Ruth Ball's enamelled pieces were often flamboyantly exotic, combining a wonderful mixture of different metal techniques and delicately applied painted enamel. Her use of the paisley motif and her imaginative use of repoussé and engraved edges riveted to painted centres is very recognizable as Ruth's design. This particular collection of work was very reminiscent of Indian textiles and Ruth says she was influenced by room interiors, fabrics and furnishings. Most of this decorative collection were brooches, but Ruth is also interested in three-dimensional forms and

Brooch in repoussé silver and painted enamel with gold cloisonné detail. 1989. Ruth Ball.

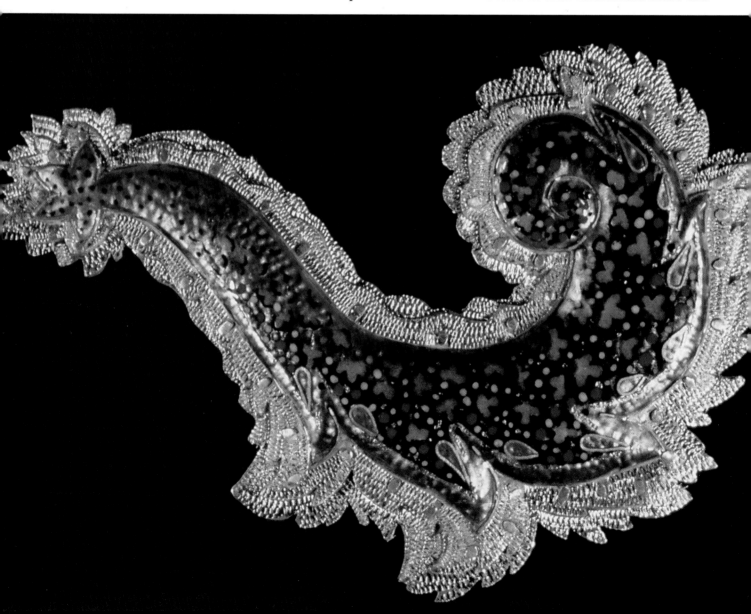

has made some perfume bottles and ornamental vessels.

Ruth often combines her enamel painting, which she does on standard silver over flux, with other enamel techniques such as champlevé and cloisonné. Her more recent pieces of jewellery are much more delicate in shape and simpler in form. Her new collection of earrings and pendant necklets is based on natural and found objects enamelled to suggest the seasons, but the concept was to make the simple leaf form the 'jewel', with its rich and glowing colours. This idea is particularly effective in the

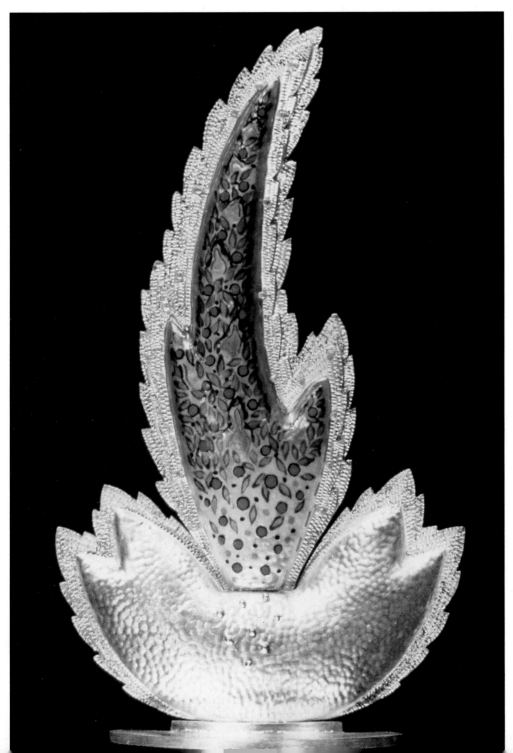

Ornamental vessel in repoussé work silver and painted enamel. 1989. Ruth Ball.

Rings in silver and enamel. 2001. Ruth Ball.

Necklaces and earrings in silver and painted enamel (winter collection). 2001. Ruth Ball.

autumn range, where the leaf forms are enamelled in the lovely pinky reds, orange yellows and tinges of pale green that appear in the season's foliage. The winter collection of pieces is enamelled in opalescent blues and silvery pale grey blues to give a cold, frosty feeling.

Her current collection of silver rings is the beginning of a new concept. She is using two painters as design inspiration, and marrying the ornate detail of Gustav Klimt with the contrasting geometry of Mondrian to formulate original ideas. She hopes in the near future to take these ideas forward to create matching designs of earrings and other pieces of jewellery. Ruth's future plans involve experimenting with larger pieces of enamel to form bigger images to extend her painting and design work, with the intention of returning to the size of her earlier work, which was so impressive.

In addition to personal work and commissions she takes part in exhibitions at Studio Fusion with the Society of British Enamellers and she exhibits regularly in the Merseyside area. Ruth teaches part time at Southport College and is a visiting lecturer in jewellery design and enamelling at the University of Lancashire on the BA (Hons) Three-Dimensional Design course.

Ruth trained at Middlesex University and gained her BA (Hons) degree in Jewellery Design. While she was in college she was fortunate to spend her work placement year employed full-time by Alan Mudd in his workshops on a variety of trade enamel pieces.

GILLIE HOYTE BYROM

Gillie Hoyte Byrom is one of the very few miniature portrait painters in Britain today who work in vitreous enamels. She exhibits annually with the Royal Society of Miniature Painters, Sculptors and Gravers at the Westminster Gallery, and was elected to full membership of this prestigious society in 1992.

Gillie made a decision to pursue a career in enamelling shortly after being introduced to the craft through a chance encounter at a craft fair in 1977. Since that time she has developed her painting techniques through research and a number of years producing flower paintings in enamel, which were made into jewellery and sold throughout the world. After twelve years Gillie found that this had become repetitive and, after a suggestion from her husband and with his encouragement, started to consider the challenge of miniature portraiture. She discovered that the Llotja School in Barcelona ran a five-year course that incorporated a section on miniature portrait painting, and was able to join the course for that particular section. This was an intense one-month training period, but she returned from Barcelona to make five tiny creations, which were exhibited at the Royal Miniaturist Society. The society was surprised at the improvement in her work and awarded her a prize for these enamels. Gillie's decision to go to Barcelona and learn the traditional methods of painting was the start of her very successful career and she felt that she had found her métier.

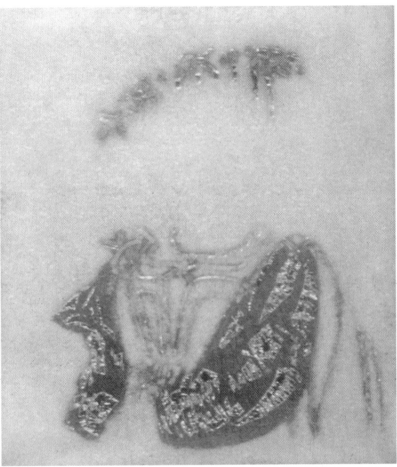

Gillie usually works from photographs and videos of her subjects, often from more than one angle for contemporary commissions, so that she can achieve exactly the detail she needs. The portraits are mainly produced on ovals of either gold or copper or occasionally silver. She uses a transparent flux both as a counter-enamel and on the front of the piece as a base for delicate opal enamel. The opal is wet packed ground enamel and fired. Gillie is in no doubt that for her this is the best enamel base as it allows the painted enamel to soak into the surface but remains glossy and often luminous, unlike painting on china, where the colours tend to stay on the surface and the quality of depth is lost. She feels that using a build-up of the opal enamel is taking the

ABOVE: Detail of plaque (left) underlay in gold and opal enamel on 18K gold. Gillie Hoyte Byrom.

LEFT: Painted enamel plaque of Edward, Prince of Wales (after Holbein). 2000. Gillie Hoyte Byrom.

process back to methods of the eighteenth-century miniature enamels that she finds so inspiring. Gillie's portraits take at least twelve firings, some as many as twenty-five, and are so intricate and detailed that she needs to use a magnifying glass and sometimes a microscope lens to paint them.

Gillie has been greatly encouraged by the Worshipful Company of Goldsmiths, and since 1995 has won the top award for enamel painting in the Craftsmanship and Design Awards Competition. Over the last two years the Goldsmiths' Company has been encouraging her to develop her techniques and to use a centuries-old Genevan method of glass layering, which gives her work a final extra layer of flux. This tones down the enamels and creates a smooth and finely polished surface to the portrait.

Gillie enjoys writing about enamelling and portrait miniatures, and she has contributed to a number of specialist books on the subject. She frequently gives lectures, demonstrations of her work and explanations of the conjunction of art and science in her work, illustrated with her collection of slides. She is a member of the Devon Guild of Craftsmen and the British Society of Enamellers, exhibiting regularly with both societies. Gillie is also a member of the Hilliard Society. She was invited in 2000 by Studio Fusion to exhibit fifty of her portrait miniatures. Many of these were commissioned pieces over the last ten years kindly loaned by clients. One of Gillie's latest portraits is that of Edward, Prince of Wales (after Holbein), 6.5 × 7.5cm, and painted on 18K gold. This won her the first prize and a Special Award in the Goldsmiths' 2001 Competition.

DAYNA WHITE

Many of Dayna White's painted enamels are delicately detailed observations of birds and their habitats. Her techniques vary slightly from piece to piece to give the detail and depth of colour she requires.

Painted enamel plaque inspired by Paul Klee. Dayna White.

*Gannets, painted
enamel plaque.*
Dayna White.

She uses both copper and silver bases, sometimes with as many as ten coats of enamel paint, while other pieces have a single layer of shaded painting on a coloured ground over an area that has been etched to give a raised border.

Dayna took a BTec Diploma in Art and Design and, instead of continuing at college, she decided to join Toye, Kenning and Spencer in the Birmingham Jewellery Quarter. This is a firm specializing in the production of enamelled badges, medals and regalia. Her training was in the traditional style of an apprenticeship and she spent two years working for the head artist, when she learnt to prepare his enamels and do very simple paintings.

After two years she progressed to working on her own and eventually took on some of the prestigious civic regalia commissions. During this period she used any quiet moments to teach herself (through reading an old enamelling book) techniques of cloisonné, plique à jour and the use of foils. Five years later, in 1992, Dayna moved to Thomas Fattorini Ltd, still in the Birmingham Jewellery Quarter. Fattorini is another firm producing civic and corporate regalia, and with this company she started training as the firm's first computer designer. In the meantime she had started her own workshop and was able to carry on with enamelling and undertake some work within the trade.

In 1998 Dayna decided to extend her knowledge of enamelling and joined a City and Guilds Course at the Jewellery Faculty of the UCE. Her course tutor was Penny Gildea, and with her enthusiasm and encouragement Dayna not only completed her year's course but in 1999 was invited to teach an evening class in enamelling at the college, which she is still doing. In 2000 Dayna left Fattorini, set up her workshop full-time and became self-employed. Now she wants to move away from accepting other people's work and concentrate on her own designs. One of her recent pieces is inspired by the painter Paul Klee and has an etched centre base with a cream ground decorated with three coats of enamel paint.

Bar brooches and cufflinks in silver, fine gold wire, gold leaf and enamel. 1994. Sheila McDonald.

LUSTRES AND FOILS

Lustres

To give added decoration and richness to painted enamels, lustres, often called liquid gold, can be painted on the surface prior to the final firing. Gold lustres are used to give definition, to sharpen the outlines and to create highlights as well as to give visual interest. Care should be taken when covering large or curved areas of enamel as, unless the lustre is applied very sparingly, a crazed surface may result. Other lustres are available that give varying effects, such as opalescent, bronze, and mother of pearl (which produces a semitransparent pearly iridescent covering).

Foils

Gold or silver can be worked into the enamelled design by using ready-prepared foils or by hammering down sheets of gold or silver.

Collection of brooches, earrings and cufflinks in hardenable silver, fine gold wire, gold leaf and enamel. 2000. Sheila McDonald.

Gold and Silver Leaf

Commercial ready-to-use gold or silver leaf is usually sold in sheets of about 7.5cm square protected between two layers of very delicate tissue paper. To start working with the leaf, first decide where it is to be on the enamelling, as it can lie on the first thin layer of fired enamel or be closer to the surface, depending on the desired final effect. Having decided on the shape and size, trace or draw it lightly on the top tissue surface, then cut out the shape with a sharp pair of small scissors, keeping the tissue-foil-tissue sandwich together. Discard the bottom layer of tissue and, using either a small drop of gum or saliva where the foil is to lie, place the foil and adjust to the exact position. Remove the remaining tissue with a damp brush or tweezers. Tilt the enamel piece slightly and, with a fine sable brush or eyedropper, touch the top corner of the foil with tap water, which will draw the water under the foil by capillary action, sticking it to the surface. If the foil is not as flat as is required, gentle patting with a piece of tissue will level it. A drop of water at both ends of the foil will create a crinkled effect. If you need to reposition the foil, add more water and float it to the correct position.

Tap water is better than pure water for this purpose as the mineral salts will assist in the adhesion.

At this stage it is possible to decorate the foil by imprinting with a blunt point or self-made punches. (Whether to prick the foil to allow air to escape is very much a personal decision.) Using overlapping gold and silver foils together can produce some interesting patterns. Because the expansion rates of the two metals are different, where they overlap they may separate and a reticulation process will start, so some areas may need burnishing down. If the design allows some of the foil to remain on the surface above the enamel, it can look very rich, but the firing has to be carefully monitored or it will melt. The American enamellist Bill Helwig uses this method on his panels with beautiful results. He sandwiches his silver and gold foil in between tracing papers, tears off strips and handles the foils into place, allowing some to overlap, and then applies layers of enamel on top.

Sheet Metal

The second method uses a rolling mill or hammering to make very thin high karat gold, pure gold or pure silver sheet. The

Necklace in hardenable silver, 18K yellow gold, gold foil and cloisonné. Jeanne Werge-Hartley.

Setting Gemstones in Enamel

Gemstone settings should have a wire surround to protect the enamel when the stone is being set, and it is advisable to have a second layer of protection by covering the enamel with masking tape. No gemstones, even diamonds, should be set before enamelling, as the impact of a sudden rise in temperature would either shatter or discolour the stone.

Laboratory-grown gemstones can be inserted into PMC before the clay is sintered and the shrinkage will hold them in place.

Dorothy has experimented with many types of enamel on copper and a variety of different silver alloys, and is making an interesting record of what is possible with these materials.

Methods

Raku enamelling involves firing thinly laid enamels onto the metal, removing the piece from the kiln as quickly as possible,

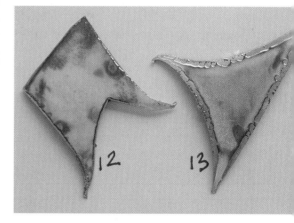

advantage of this is that the resulting pieces will not wrinkle as the foil does, and it is possible to chase fine lines, or design more complex patterns than is possible on the purchased foil. After applying the decoration, anneal to ensure that the metal is soft and can be flattened without affecting the lines, then proceed to lay it on the metal or enamel as with the foil. This is a good method of solving the design problem of covering unsightly solder seams. A large area can be covered in small units of the foil to create a mosaic, which makes a good background for transparent enamels and red in particular.

RAKU

A recent interest in the Japanese ceramic art form raku, using enamels on metal rather than on clay, has produced some very beautiful lustres. Dorothy Cockrell, an enameller in Edinburgh, was introduced to this method of working at an international symposium in Bristol with Elizabeth Turrell. Since then Dorothy has been producing test pieces that are quite different from any other form of enamelling. As with ceramic raku, the results are totally dependent on the basic material, the applied enamel and the contents of the reducing bin, so there is always an element of surprise in the final outcome.

TOP: *Three pieces of standard silver, covered with flux (Soyer silver, Thompson lead-free and Supersoft), fired and plunged into newspaper.* Dorothy Cockrell.

MIDDLE: *Britannia silver, fluxed twice (in liquid flux and 232) and plunged into newspaper.* Dorothy Cockrell.

BOTTOM: *Fine silver/copper plate, fired with liquid flux and plunged into newspaper.* Dorothy Cockrell.

putting it directly into the reducing bin and rapidly placing a lid firmly on top. The hot enamel incinerates the contents and the tight lid prevents the oxygen from being replaced, which creates the reducing atmosphere and produces the lustre. The contents of the bin are limited only by the imagination. Damp newspaper gives a smooth surface, organic materials, such as leaves, pine needles, lavender or cattle droppings create textured finishes. Sawdust can be used to give texture, although care must be taken as prior treatment to the wood may cause toxic fumes. Dorothy records an interesting test recently with seaweed and also reports of a potter using nettles from a polluted industrial site which produced wonderful colours. Tim McCreight discusses another method of raku firing with Precious Metal Clay in his book *Working with Precious Metal Clay*. A great deal of exciting and individual experimentation is being carried out in this field, but the research in its application to make bowls, plates, tiles, vases and jewellery needs further investigation.

SHEILA R. MCDONALD

The enamel jewellery of Sheila McDonald is reminiscent of the detailed embroideries and lavishly appliquéd costumes of the Russian ballets such as the *Firebird* and *Scheherazade*. She uses silver, often 1715 hardenable silver, overlaid with brilliant transparent pinks, blues and turquoises contrasting with bands of black or dark blue enamel, all of which are embellished with triangles and circles of fine gold leaf and zigzags of pure gold wire. It is not surprising to discover that she originally studied textile design at Glasgow School of Art for one year before changing to the silversmithing and jewellery course. The time studying textiles, she says, has proved to be a strong influence in her work. She works from coloured source sketches using watercolour to represent the vibrancy that she subsequently achieves in her jewellery. At the Royal College of Art she started to become interested in enamels and did some plique à jour pieces and a little painted enamel with Keith Seddon,

Bar brooches in silver, fine gold wire, gold leaf and enamel. 1994. Sheila McDonald.

Brooches in silver, fine gold and enamel with chased silver detail. Sheila McDonald.

Monochromatic brooches in hardenable and standard silver, fine gold and silver leaf with enamel. Sheila McDonald. 1998.

although she says she already did some experimenting on copper in a small kiln when she was about thirteen.

Her brooches, which are rounded triangular shapes, are enamelled in stripes, have triangles and small squares of gold leaf decoration, and are given a three-dimensional interest by the addition of a sweeping chased silver plume. Sheila admits many of her ideas, including these plume brooches, arrive when she is sketching while she is on the telephone; she is then able to develop these subconscious influences into interesting and final solutions.

Her more monochromatic pieces were made for a specific exhibition at the Scottish Gallery and are quite different to her other work. In these pieces she has been fascinated by devoré velvet, where the background is etched away. By using layers of one enamel colour and trapping silver and gold leaf between to create the patterns, Sheila is creating a similar look to the fabric in her brooches. These pieces are an interesting departure from her previous work and she hopes to develop this idea further. Like many other designers Sheila responds well to the stimulus of being asked to work to a themed exhibition or commission.

Sheila has exhibited widely in England and Scotland since 1985, at Electrum in London, Leeds Art Gallery, the V&A Museum London, and numerous Dazzle exhibitions. Sheila has been a member of the British Society of Enamellers since its inception in 1987 and has exhibited with them since that time both in the UK and abroad. She sells her jewellery through thirteen galleries in England and Scotland and has work in collections at Goldsmiths' Hall and four other major art galleries. In 1990 she was granted the Freedom of the Worshipful Company of Goldsmiths.

DOROTHY COCKRELL

Dorothy enjoys pushing the boundaries of conventional enamelling techniques and finds experimenting and discovery just as satisfying as producing a finished piece. Her recent forays into enamel raku have produced some fascinating results. Plunging hot-fired enamels and fluxes straight from the kiln into tins containing obscure materials produce lustres that are often very beautiful and quite different from normal fired enamel.

Dorothy attended jewellery evening classes at Edinburgh College of Art while she was involved in general teaching and was introduced to enamelling by Jane Short at a West Dean College short course. She has been enamelling full-time since retiring from teaching in the mid 1980s and has gained her craftsman status and other awards from the Guild of Enamellers. She now edits the Guild's newsletters and runs workshops at their conferences. She is an Associate member of the British Society of Enamellers and was invited to exhibit her work in a major enamelling exhibition in 2001 at the Bilston Craft Gallery.

Brooch (60mm × 70mm) in silver and cloisonné (adapted from a nineteenth-century Chinese cabinet). Dorothy Cockrell.

8 ENAMELLING ON CURVED SURFACES

This chapter deals with beads, finger rings and other specialist three-dimensional objects and the problems of applying enamel in the round.

BEADS

Beads have been a way of decorating the body since cave dwellers crudely polished up pebbles to adorn themselves, and today many enamellers are producing the most beautiful unusual shapes and sizes of bead. While some craftsmen make their own beads, others buy manufactured ones to avoid having a solder seam and to focus their attention on the enamelling process. Beads can be any shape, from a perfect round or oval to those with an angular form or irregular shape. The biggest problem is avoiding solder seams, which are difficult to cover with enamel because the colour either becomes discoloured or the enamel pings off as it cools down after being brought out of the kiln. Incorporating thin or decorative wires, foil or applied solid shapes are ways of covering these joins and can become an innovative addition to the overall design of the bead.

Necklace of silver enamel beads textured with gold foil alternating with Sugulith beads. 2001. Joan MacKarell.

*Necklace of silver
enamelled beads and gold
beads. The enamelled
beads are decorated with
cabochon garnets,
pure gold foil and
gold granulation. In the
collection of the Worshipful
Company of Goldsmiths.
Ruth Rushby.*

Making the Bead

Round and oval beads are usually domed up in two halves in a doming block, then soldered with enamelling solder to make a complete bead; a hole has to be drilled to allow the hot air to escape. One way to avoid a large area of solder appearing on the surface of the bead is to make an inner curved bezel that will friction fit the two halves. If this is done really tightly it may be sufficient to hold the two parts together; if not, two very thin areas of solder run round the curved bezel will hold them and, as the centre seam is almost invisible, burnishing the seam may eliminate it. Putting a layer of silver or gold foil over the seam and under the enamel will hide it totally. Usually a thin wire circle is soldered round the hole where the chain or cord will pass through.

Cylindrical beads are made by constructing a tube of the required size, or using a manufactured tube cut to length. The ends can be closed by soldering either a flat end with a hole for threading or a small dome shape, which can have a loop added to hang the bead from or attach it to the next bead. A friction fit end is also possible if a flat wire is soldered on to the side of the dome that faces the tube.

An angular shape, such as a rectangular or square bead, can be made by scoring and bending, the inside seams strengthened by flowing solder down them and the ends finished as with the cylinder beads. The scope of this method is enormous and the limit is only determined by the technical ability and the imagination of the maker.

The metal thickness used for the bead will vary according to the size and type of metal used – usually 14 gauge will be sufficient in standard silver, about 20 gauge in pure silver and as thin as 8 gauge if hardenable silver is used. If the bead is to be engraved before enamelling the metal should be thicker than normal. Some craftsmen prefer to counter-enamel the inside of the bead, and this can be done with a powder enamel diluted to a thin, creamy solution. Block one end of the bead and pass the enamel into the bead using a pipette or eye dropper. Swill it around for a minute or two, then pour out the residue and dry before starting to decorate the outside. (For making beads using PMC, *see* Chapter 10.)

friction fit bead

*circle of wire round
bead opening*

*cylinder bead with
friction fit cap*

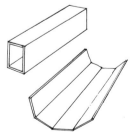

*construction of square
or rectangular bead*

Bead constructions.

Necklace of silver and enamel beads with gold foil, box snap set with turquoise. Joan MacKarell.

Enamelling the Bead

If there are no cloisons or engraving to assist the enamel to hold to the curved surface, a thin layer of Klyrfyre or gum tragacanth sifted onto the bead may be used. Cloisonné beads need to have the wires curved in two directions to fit the bead and they must be held securely to it while the enamel is being wet packed. This can be achieved by dipping the bead into gum tragacanth and securing it in a thin layer of flux, or by soldering it with a minimal amount of solder (*see* Chapter 3). When the enamel is wet laid it should be blotted to stop it slipping round the bead or dropping off altogether. Water tension will keep the enamel in position on larger vases as well as on small beads, as long as the enamel is kept damp – by applying a minute drop of pure water at intervals with a fine paintbrush – while the piece is revolved. There is a fine balance between being too dry or too wet. As in all enamelling the best

Detail of necklace shown on page 108. Alexandra Raphael.

Handmade silver chain with enamelled silver beads decorated with 18K gold wire, and enamelled drop inset with fine gold wires. Ruth Rushby.

results are achieved when two or three thin coats are applied rather than one thick one.

Firing the Bead

Consider very carefully how to support the bead while it is in the kiln as any movement may spill the dry enamel. One method is to use iron wire threaded through the bead and then support the wire between an M-shaped piece of mesh or trivet. The firing needs to be done as quickly as possible at just below 1000°C (1832°F). After the bead has been cleaned in dilute sulphuric acid it must be washed thoroughly in a solution of bicarbonate of soda to ensure that no acid is left inside the bead.

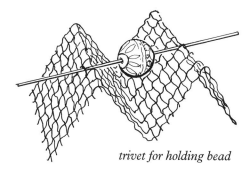

trivet for holding bead

Enamelled beads with Indian agate beads. 1999. Penny Gildea.

RINGS, BANGLES, WHISTLES AND PENS

Enamel can be added to a finger ring, bangle or napkin ring in a number of ways, from introducing a small area of colour to covering the entire piece with enamel. If the piece is to remain in its original shape when worn or used, the first consideration is the thickness and strength of the metal, as, if the metal is too thin, the shape can easily be bent, whereupon the enamel will crack and possibly fall out. The solder join of the ring is an area vulnerable to the discolouring or rejection of the enamel, or the possibility of the seam coming apart in the kiln. One effective way of coping with this is to design the piece so that either wire or a small piece of sheet is placed on top to stop

LEFT: *Pens in 18K white and yellow gold with champlevé.* Phil Barnes.

BELOW: *Rings in hardenable silver, 18K gold and cloisonné.* Jeanne Werge-Hartley.

BOTTOM: *Rings in 18K gold and cloisonné.* Fred Rich.

the solder showing. Alternatively you can apply a rim to stop the join coming apart by soldering a flat piece of sheet metal to the top and bottom of the ring, with an external overlap to give an edge, and removing the centre by saw piercing. This will hold the ring solder joint intact and ensures that there is no solder join on the rim – and it also gives a good finished top and bottom edge for enamelling.

Solder ring to bottom sheet and saw-pierce out centre of ring.

Solder on to bottom sheet and saw-pierce centre of ring.

Saw off the outside sheet leaving a seamless rim.

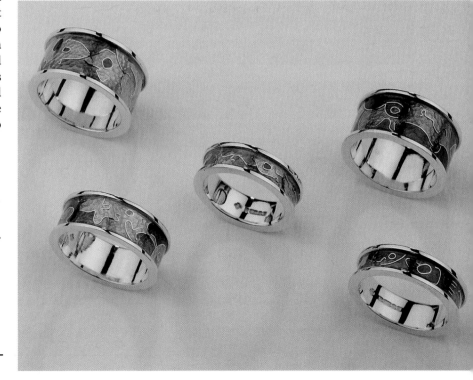

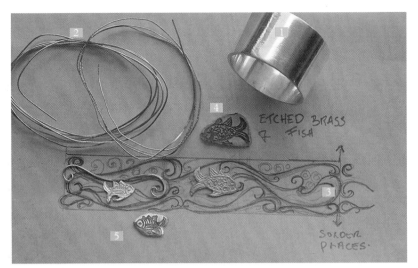

Stages of making silver, 18K and enamel ring. 2001. Jeanne Werge-Hartley.

1   Basic silver ring
2   Silver and 18K cloisonné
3   Working drawing
4   Etched brass fish for imprinting
5   Imprinted 18K fish

Further details of ring.

1   Working drawing
2   Soldered wires
3   The wires bent round and soldered into a circle to fit on the ring
4   Soldered on to ring

FAR LEFT: Laying in the wet enamel.
LEFT: Ring being fired.

ABOVE: Three views of finished ring.

BELOW: Rings in hardenable silver, 18K gold and enamel. Jeanne Werge-Hartley.

BELOW RIGHT: Rings in hardenable silver, 18K gold and cloisonné. Jeanne Werge-Hartley.

The alternative is to use seamless tubing, which can be purchased in many ring sizes and napkin ring shapes. These are usually 12 gauge. If needed a rim can be added for further strength and decoration. If hardenable silver is used (*see* Chapter 3), the ring should be temporarily soldered to true up the shape, hardened in the kiln and, once cool, the solder join cleaned and resoldered as the two hours in the kiln will have weakened the join. Because of the strength of this silver it is possible to use a thinner gauge. Another method for applying small areas of enamel to a larger napkin ring is to shape the ring and the individual plaques separately, solder rivets on to the back of the plaques and enamel these smaller pieces, then finally rivet them on to the ring or bangle.

Enamelling in the Round

All the usual preparations are necessary to enamel in the round, and, as with beads, the first layer should be thin and kept damp to ensure that the enamel stays on the surface as it is revolved to be filled. It should then be dried on the top of the kiln and fired. Other thin layers may be applied as necessary with further firings.

Silver, 18K gold and red enamel over platinum. Jeanne Werge-Hartley.

Polishing

Hand polishing is the safest method to finish any three-dimensional enamel piece (*see* Chapter 3). Cleaning the inside of rings can be done with a rounded piece of Garriflex abrasive to remove any firestain, followed by a flexi-drive with descending grades of emery paper slotted into its mandrel, and a calico mop used with hyfin or tripoli. Then the piece should be washed in hot, soapy water and ammonia, given a final polish with a swansdown mop and rouge, washed again and finally put to dry in fine sawdust.

RUTH RUSHBY

Ruth started enamelling whilst taking her degree in jewellery at the Central School of Art and Design when she realized how much the colourful medium had to offer and how it would allow her to expand and explore her ideas for surface decoration. She was totally intrigued by the ability to trap gold and silver wires within layers of differently coloured enamels, using opaque colours in her first pieces, but later using transparents and sometimes combining the two. Ruth always draws the basis of her ideas in her sketchbook and transfers her designs directly to the metal by laying down the patterns in silver and gold wires. She finds this process is very much like putting a pencil to paper and, as she lays the wires on the silver, the design takes on its own momentum. This preparation can take a whole day and, having covered it to keep off the dust, she returns to the piece the following morning to prepare and wet pack the enamels, often using as many as twelve colours.

Penny Whistle 'Blowing a Kiss' in silver, fine gold and silver wires with cloisonné. 2000. Penny Gildea.

It was a group of cloisonné enamel boxes that Ruth designed and made in her final year at the Royal College of Art in 1987 that first attracted attention to her work. Since that time she has exhibited widely and had several prestigious commissions, including a badge of office for the Bankers' Overseas Club, London, an enamelled bead necklace in the collection of the Worshipful Company of Goldsmiths in London and a Medal in the British Museum collection. Ruth's awards include the Prize of the City of Geneva in 1988 for an enamelled box. The list of exhibitions that Ruth has participated in is both extensive and impressive, and as one of the founder members of the Society of British Enamellers she has exhibited with them in many venues both in Britain and abroad. Recently she was invited and took part in 'Treasures of the Twentieth Century' at Goldsmiths' Hall. Originally Ruth used a palette of many colours, often combining opaques and transparents, using foils and silver wires trapped between the enamel layers.

Cone-shaped boxes in silver, gold wires and cloisonné.
Ruth Rushby.

Detail of necklace on page 133, showing the silver, gold and garnet beads. 1991.
Ruth Rushby.

Her recent work has changed and her colour palette is much reduced. Often she uses just one colour that will emphasize the form of the piece rather than merely decorate the surface. Her most recent piece is enamelled in one very beautiful soft grey, which, when fired and ground back as far as possible without breaking through to the silver beneath, and combined with the silver and detailed fine gold wires, has a subtlety of grey tones that are delicate and appealing.

Enamel has always played an important part in Ruth's work, either in a highly detailed 'storytelling' design or, as in recent pieces, adding a subtle dimension. She says:

> For me that is the beauty of the beast, because after all it has to be said that at times it can be a frustrating journey with its inherent technical difficulties, but ultimately there is no substitute for enamel: it is entirely unique in both application and in the range and quality of finish.

Ruth is co-organizer and Senior Lecturer at the London Guildhall University on the Silversmithing, Jewellery and Allied Crafts BA course.

PENNY GILDEA

Penny originally trained and gained her City and Guilds Certificate in costume jewellery, and she only began enamelling after attending the School of Jewellery in Birmingham, where she learned to engrave. Previously she had been to several of Jane Short's weekend enamelling courses at West Dean College, and it was while she

RIGHT: A series of silver necklaces with enamelled beads that have pure gold fused into the enamel surface and carved amber beads inlayed with silver wire. 2000. Ruth Rushby.

FAR RIGHT: Penny Whistle 'Blowing a Kiss' in silver, with fine gold wires and cloisonné. 2001. Penny Gildea.

was at West Dean that she was pointed towards Birmingham School of Jewellery. Penny felt that engraving skills were a new direction for her, making enamelling even more interesting, and she now works almost exclusively in silver using basse taille, champlevé and cloisonné techniques to make small objects and jewellery. In 1998 she became the Chairman of the Guild of Enamellers and she has won several of the Guild's awards. She has recently become an associate member of the British Society of Enamellers.

Although Penny continues to design and make jewellery, and uses her engraving skills to give light, contrast and depth to her colours, she has recently found a very personal theme and has started to make and exhibit a series of delightful and unusual whistles, which are both functional and decorative. Her first ones were made entirely by hand, but now she has the mouthpieces and finials cast from her own master moulds. The cloisons on the main part of the whistles are in fine gold and silver wire and the silk cord thread on which they hang is made using the Japanese Kumihimo method. These silk cords are braided in colours that harmonize with and complement the colours of the enamels on the whistle. Penny gives the whistles intriguing names such as penny whistle 'Blowing a Kiss', which has overtones of Klimt's painting, *The Kiss*. A second group of whistles, called Simple Penny Whistles, are enamelled in one colour over an engraved surface with a matching silk Kumihimo braid. The whistles work, and Penny says:

> Why not wear a whistle as a piece of jewellery in its own right, then, when calling the dogs or children, drowning the voice of an unwelcome caller, bringing the boardroom back to the agenda or calling time in the pub, do it with wit, style, panache and a penny whistle.

JOAN MACKARELL

Joan MacKarell was born in County Donegal in Ireland and, after graduating from Belfast School of Art with a National Diploma in Design in Woven and Printed Textiles, went to Liverpool School of Art to take an Art Teachers' Diploma. Joan's love of colour in both her paintings and her enamels results from her textile training and her childhood memories of the North Atlantic Irish landscape, wild seas

LEFT: *Silver and cloisonné pendant, which opens to hold an amulet.* Joan MacKarell.

BELOW: *Pebble box (60 × 25mm) in silver and enamel.* Joan MacKarell.

Necklace of silver and textured underfired beads with Dumorterite beads and red coral, and ear studs in enamel, coral and Rhodonite. 2001. Joan MacKarell.

and ever-changing huge skies. She also remembers as a child the excitement of opening mysterious parcels sent by relatives from India and discovering colourful textiles, intricate metal jewellery and other fascinating items which she thinks must have kindled her interest both in the exotic and in miniature art.

Joan feels her work is about odyssey, in that it is rooted in human experience and contains a large degree of observation and intimacy. She feels that enamel allows her to express and fulfil all her passions. Joan started to be interested in enamelling after she had attended a short ILEA course for teachers. She was inspired by the colours and the possibilities of telling a story in metal, and in 1983 she went on a course at Sir John Cass College in London because she wanted to use enamels on jewellery and three-dimensional forms.

In the last ten years Joan's enamel pieces have been on exhibition in Japan, the United States, Canada, Ireland, France and Spain. In Britain she has exhibited widely with the British Society of Enamellers, and in the Goldsmiths' Hall Craft Council Competition in 1986 she won an award in the design section. She is an active co-director of Studio Fusion. Joan has her enamels in a number of collections, including those of the Worshipful Company of Dyers, the Museum in Geneva and the Gilbert Collection in Somerset House, London, for which she designed a box in enamel and silver. Joan was instrumental in forming the British Society of Enamellers and was a founder executive member in 1985.

Her recent work is about colour and texture and is heavily influenced by her painting forays in Portugal and by patterns and colours revealed by layering through time and the elements. Her most recent bead necklaces and earrings are in a soft and nectareous range of underfired enamel and are very tactile. Joan calls the stud earrings her 'fondants', but the necklace beads are quite unique, lovely and very covetable.

MAUREEN EDGAR

Maureen Edgar is an established artist enameller whose talented work is represented in both public and private collections, including the Worshipful Company of Goldsmiths, the Scottish Crafts Council and the Royal Museum of Scotland's twentieth-century collection. She trained at Dundee School of Art, followed by

three years at the Royal College of Art, where she gained her Masters degree.

Maureen uses enamel on sterling silver, and regards weight as important an element of her design as the visual and tactile qualities. She uses both champlevé and cloisonné techniques and, by using engraved surfaces under a number of layers of enamel, she achieves greater density and clear jewel colours. All her work is hand polished and the enamelled areas are finished with various etched surfaces.

In 1976 Maureen was commended in the Diamonds International Awards. In 1980 and 1981 she exhibited her work in Enamels International in London and Germany and in Best of British Enterprises in London, while in 1982 her work was in

Enamelled vase with geese design. 1990. Maureen Edgar.

Cockatoo pepper mill in silver and enamel. 1990. Maureen Edgar.

an SDA Scottish promotion in Japan, and in 1984 in Limoges, France.

A very striking silver and enamel vase made in 1990 depicts white geese and delicate plant life against a beautiful background. This was displayed at Goldsmiths' Hall in 1994 in the Art of Enamelling exhibition. Also displayed in this prestigious exhibition was a Cockatoo pepper mill, predominantly enamelled in white and a vibrant turquoise blue over an engraved surface. The yellow of the cockatoo's comb is a lovely contrast and gives the mill an interesting focal point. A piece made for a private collection in 1996 is an 18K gold enamelled compact, the design of which is based on a yellow and green fish swimming through underwater flora on a blue background, engraved to give the feeling of reflecting water.

In 1989 Maureen was made a Freeman of the Worshipful Company of Goldsmiths.

Compact in gold and enamel. 1996. Maureen Edgar.

9 PRECIOUS METAL CLAY

DEFINITION AND HISTORY

This interesting and revolutionary precious material is the result of many years of research by Dr Morikawa, a metallurgist and director of a state-of-the-art refining facility that is part of the Mitsubishi Corporation in Sanda, Japan. The clay was introduced to Britain in 1995 through the London branch of the Mitsubishi Materials Corporation, who invited a few established jewellers to experiment with the material before launching it on the British jewellery scene. Jewellers in the USA, led by Tim McCreight, had already discovered its potential and it was creating much interest among the jewellers and ceramists there. Since 1996 a number of British craftsmen have been working with the clay and PMC lectures and workshops have been initiated through conferences and in college programmes.

PMC is a composition of precious metal – silver or gold powder of less than twenty microns – mixed with water and an organic binder. This mix gives the material the properties of porcelain clay and it can be modelled and used in similar ways. After being dried the PMC piece is fired in a kiln, a process called sintering, to burn out the organic binder of the material and any remaining water. When this process is complete the result is pure precious metal

Precious Metal Clay products.

1 *Pack of Precious Metal Clay sheet*
2 *Pack of Precious Metal Clay Plus*
3 *Syringe of Precious Metal Clay slip*

of hallmarking quality that is smaller in size than the original.

INTRODUCTION TO THE MATERIAL

When a piece has been made in PMC it has to be allowed to dry, and the time taken will depend on the size and mass of the piece. Protected from contamination, it may be left to dry naturally, which may take several days, or dried more rapidly with a hot air blower or in a kiln at 120°C (250°F). In its dry state there is no limit to its shelf life, as long as it is protected against physical damage. If you are not sure whether the PMC is totally dry it is necessary to place the PMC in a cold kiln and raise the temperature slowly to 120°C (250°F) to allow the remaining water to vaporize and then take the heat up to the sintering temperature.

Once the clay is totally dry, place it on a support in the kiln, raise the temperature to sintering level and hold it there for at least the period recommended, so that the metal particles fuse together and the water and binder evaporate. It may be left longer at this temperature, but undersintering will leave a weak metal. When the sintering is complete remove the piece from the kiln and quench it in water. When PMC was first introduced, the sintering process was very lengthy and the exact temperatures had to be arrived at in steps with thirty-minute intervals until the piece was fully sintered, a matter of seven hours in total. However, more research and developmental work has been done and the hours in the kiln have been reduced drastically. The newest PMC Plus can be sintered in ten minutes with much the same results.

Depending on the length of sintering time the piece will shrink by degrees; using standard PMC this would have reduced the surface area by 30 per cent and the volume by 50 per cent. Recently the

PMC Firing Times

Original silver PMC
2 hours minimum at 900°C (1650°F)
Shrinkage at 2 hours: 24 per cent

There are various sintering times for PMC Plus and PMC3

Silver PMC Plus
Shrinkage at 30 minutes: 13.7 per cent
10 minutes at 900°C (1650°F)
20 minutes at 850°C (1560°F)
30 minutes at 800°C (1470°F)

Silver PMC3
Shrinkage at 30 minutes 12.7 per cent
10 minutes at 700°C (1290°F)
20 minutes at 650°C (1200°F)
30 minutes at 600°C (1100°F)

Pure Gold PMC
Shrinkage at 2 hours: approx. 40 per cent
2 hours minimum at 1000°C (1830°F)

shrinking has become more controllable and, because it can be sintered in the kiln for shorter lengths of time, the reduction need only be as much as the designer requires. Like reducing drawings by photocopying, the results are an enhanced and ultra precise version of the original.

DESIGNING FOR PMC

Forget the metallic aspects when beginning to use PMC as they tend to limit ideas. Treat it as a clay and use it in a freer way, rather than with the rigid constraints of metal. In order to use the clay effectively, start from the premise that you can make things that would not be possible in metal: this challenging thought can lead to intriguing discoveries and totally new concepts. When working out ideas it helps to have materials like plasticine or ceramic clay to practise on before embarking on work in PMC. Like any other material, PMC has advantages and disadvantages, and if used in an unsympathetic way it can get a rather poor reputation. Unfortunately it can be seen as a quick method of making lots of very ordinary objects, which could quite easily be made from other materials. Generally speaking, many of the simple results could also be achieved by casting, but the advantage of PMC is that it has a spontaneity and is almost immediate, whereas casting goes through a number of often lengthy processes, particularly if there are undercuts, when casting is often not a viable proposition from a technical viewpoint. It is possible to make an interesting master in PMC from which to cast multiples.

METHODS OF WORKING THE CLAY

PMC needs to be tightly wrapped in cling film when not being used for, although it is possible to reconstitute dried PMC with water, it is preferable not to allow it to dry out. Before starting to use the clay add a few drops of water and knead it to make it soft and malleable while it is still wrapped in the cling film. When using it take only the amount required out of the wrapping and, to ensure that none is wasted, rub a vegetable oil such as olive oil into your hands so that the PMC does not adhere to your skin.

PMC can be rolled by hand, shaped, pinched, twisted, cut into shapes and extruded through syringes or bakers' tubes. It can be pushed into rubber moulds for making repeating shapes and formed round polystyrene, papier mâché and wax to form hollow beads and three-dimensional shapes.

It can be combined with other materials, imprinted with almost anything to produce patterned surfaces, mixed with enamel powder and, once sintered, can be soldered, enamelled and hallmarked in the same way as any fine silver.

If a flat piece of PMC is required it can be rolled out on a perspex sheet, using a length of wooden dowel or a rigid plastic tube as a rolling pin. Using two pieces of card as spacers, roll the PMC between them to a uniform thickness, which will depend on the depth of the card, while remembering that the thickness created will shrink during sintering. The flat piece can be cut to size, shaped and joined to other shapes with a little water or PMC slip.

You can also roll the PMC between a rigid plastic board and a rectangular block of smooth wood to form thin cylindrical wires, which can be coiled and shaped to form raised decoration and attached to the main piece with a small amount of water or slip. Thinner wires can be achieved by extruding clay through a syringe or bakers' tubes. Grains or small solid beads can be made by rolling tiny lumps of PMC between well-oiled palms and placing the granulation onto a prepared area with slip using a small paintbrush.

Decoration can be applied at any stage, and modelling tools, scalpels, paintbrushes

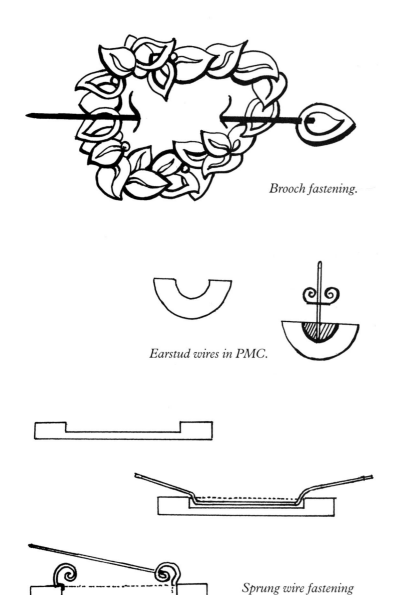

Brooch fastening.

Earstud wires in PMC.

Sprung wire fastening embedded in PMC.

SINTERING

A thermostatically controlled kiln is recommended to sinter the PMC. It is critical to hold the silver clay at 900°C (1650°F) and the gold at 1000°C (1830°F), as above these temperatures the metal will melt. The clay should be placed on a support suitable for the heat so that you can move it easily in and out of the kiln, or laid in a loose powder if you are firing a three-dimensional piece. Kiln supports may be any of the following: bisque tiles (available through pottery suppliers); enamelling fibreboards; very thin sheets of mica placed on a steel mesh; thin sections of soft firebrick not less than 2.5cm thick; or terracotta plant pot bases sold in garden centres. This last support can also be used to contain the loose materials that will hold the three-dimensional items, such as beads. This loose material can be alumina powder as used on kiln shelves in potteries; vermiculite, which is a form of mica and can be bought in garden centres and hardware stores; dry plaster of Paris; investment powder used in jewellery casting processes; or grog, the fired ceramic material that looks similar to sand.

FINDINGS AND FIXINGS

Jewellers' findings is the name given to those fittings that enable the piece to be worn, such as brooch fastenings. Soldering findings onto PMC is possible, although you have to be careful to make sure that the porous area that is to be soldered is burnished or tumbled with steel shot to prevent the solder from sinking into the PMC and making a poor connection. The soldering process must be done as quickly as possible, heating the whole piece and stopping as soon as the solder begins to flow. Flow the solder first on to the finding that is to be added, place it on the burnished area with flux and then heat the PMC quickly to draw the solder down to make a good contact.

and other articles that produce decorative patterns can all be used with the material, either in its soft state or when it is leather hard, as with green porcelain. Any small fragments that are carved off should be collected and placed in a container with water. In time this will form a slip that can be used in many different ways, such as joining parts together or painting in layers over a former.

It is much easier to design a piece when the fastenings are either integral or are embedded in the PMC, for example the fastening pin can be curved to go through the clothing or a sprung wire pin can be embedded in the back of the PMC and secured by the firing process. In this method the piece needs to be well supported on a fibreboard or a carved hole in firebrick. Ear wires can also be embedded in PMC. In order to preserve the decoration on the front while attaching the back findings, allow the piece to become leather hard, carve out an area into which the findings will fit, put some fresh soft PMC into the hollow and insert the findings. Allow the PMC to become leather hard, pass the ear wire through a hole in a piece of mica, place on a wire mesh tray and protect the silver wire with Diewersol and sinter. To regain the hardness of the ear wire gently tap the wire with a small hammer or hold the wire with snipe pliers as close as possible to the back of the earring and, with another pair of pliers, gently twist the wire until it is rigid.

Back Fastenings for Brooches

An easier platform to enable brooch findings to be soldered can be achieved by embedding a smaller piece of pure silver sheet into the back of the PMC brooch before sintering. Make this piece smaller than the brooch to allow for the shrinkage of the PMC.

Linking Units Together

When making individual pieces to be linked together as a chain or when making a pendant, the opening where the link will be can be incorporated into the design to save you drilling a hole in the unit. An interesting shape can be cut out of PMC sheet separately and added to make a decorative feature of the opening.

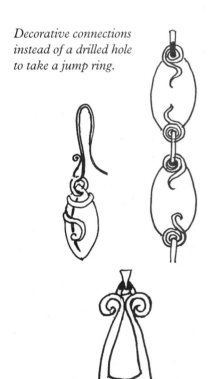

Decorative connections instead of a drilled hole to take a jump ring.

Making a PMC chain.

Make individual links, sinter and saw through alternate links (A) and open them sufficiently to pass links (B) through. Close and add a layer of thin PMC slip, sinter, then file and polish.

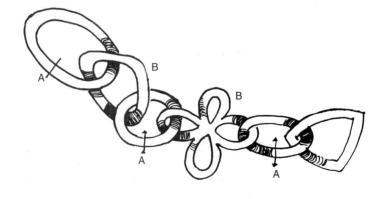

OPPOSITE PAGE:
PMC and hardenable silver chain (no soldering). Jeanne Werge-Hartley.

RIGHT: Section of enamelled PMC and hardenable silver chain. Jeanne Werge-Hartley.

FAR RIGHT: Pure gold PMC and platinum. Jeanne Werge-Hartley.

FINISHING

When the piece comes out of the kiln it has a white surface. You can leave this and simply burnish the highlights or polish the deposit away with sandpapers and buffs as with normal silver. Alternatively you can put the finished piece in a tumble polisher, sandblast it, or finish it with a steel or brass brush. Even when the piece is sintered and has turned into pure metal an amount of finishing can still be done with dental burrs in a flexi-drive and with engraving tools. It is possible to use liver of sulphur to oxidize the surface and polish the patina to give emphasis to the pattern.

USING HARDENABLE SILVER WITH PMC

If 1715 hardenable wire can be used, the problem of linking can be made easier and much more interesting. The hardenable silver can be shaped, hardened and attached to the unfired PMC shapes, as once the PMC is sintered it will shrink and hold the wires tightly in place. If the wires are polished prior to embedding, very little polishing will be necessary when the whole piece is finished. It is also possible to place pieces of 1715 hardenable silver between two pieces of PMC before sintering to make a three-dimensional piece without using solder.

Gold PMC

This can be used in exactly the same way as silver, the main disadvantage being the expense. However, it can be incorporated into a larger silver form in small pieces as either simple decoration, or as an area to be enamelled. It bonds and sinters with silver PMC at 900°C (1650°F), although on its own it needs to be fired and sintered at 1000°C (1830°F).

Pleated hardenable silver held between two imprinted parts of PMC prior to sintering. Jeanne Werge-Hartley.

Sintered PMC and silver. Jeanne Werge-Hartley.

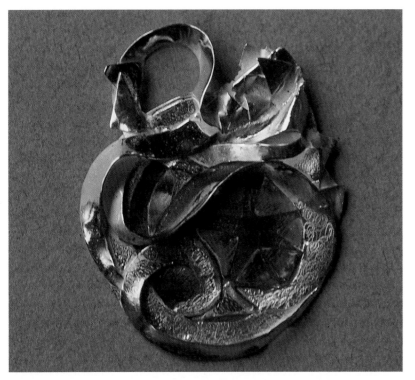

ENAMELLING ON PMC

As the sintered PMC is pure metal there are no major technical problems to overcome to enamel the finished piece. The metal tends to be porous, as with cast units, and it is advisable to burnish and seal the pores before packing the wet enamel, but otherwise the enamelling methods are the same.

It is interesting to rethink the methodology of producing an enamel piece in PMC to reflect the plastic qualities of the material and not to try to imitate what can be achieved using ordinary silver sheet and wire. One of the possibilities of PMC is to achieve the look of fabric, with all the potential of folds and soft drapes. To embellish this idea with enamel colours could produce a totally new look and variation of the enamelling process. Another method of introducing enamel into PMC is to knead dry enamel grains into the wet clay, moulding the clay into shapes and either adding texture or using it as a decorative addition to a larger piece of work before sintering. Experience has shown that using PMC Plus and making sure the piece is totally dry gives better results, so that the sintering is as fast as possible to ensure that the enamel mixed in the clay does not overfire and burn out. Certain colours react better than others and it is worth experimenting with small quantities to begin with. Enamel powder sprinkled into patterned recesses of the wet PMC can give an unusual effect when sintered.

ABOVE: PMC sheet and enamel. Jeanne Werge-Hartley.

BELOW: PMC with enamel powder kneaded in prior to sintering. Jeanne Werge-Hartley.

ENAMELLED BEADS IN PMC

Making beads and imprinting them with detail, which can then be enamelled after sintering, is another variation that has potential, not only in the variety of shapes that are possible but also in the application of the enamel. The variations of shapes of beads to enamel have no limitations.

The basic premise in bead making in PMC is that a 'core' of a material, which will burn out in the kiln, will give the basic shape and by sintering produce the bead at a reduced size. Any material that will burn out in the kiln can be used as a core, however unusual it may seem to be. It is worth looking at an American website, www.pmcguild.com, which has a series of message boards that allow American craftsmen to contact each other with new ideas for the use of PMC. The messages about core materials for beads are fascinating in the variety of things being used. They list various sorts of cereals, such as cornflakes,

and in this case the core material is coated with a thin layer of wax to help the PMC to adhere. The message boards also have useful information about raku on PMC.

Making a Bead

A core can be made out of paper clay or papier mâché. Roll the PMC out as a flat piece and cut and shape enough clay to fit round the core. If the bead is spherical, two circles of PMC can be formed into hemispheres round the core, joined at the 'equator' and sealed with a little water or slip. Leave the bead to dry (the amount of time needed for this will depend on the temperature of the workshop and the weight of the material), then carry out any imprinting. Once the PMC is leather hard the decoration can be refined with a scalpel or scraper. When the bead is completely dry place it in the kiln in the loose support material and sinter, during which process the core burns away and the hollow bead is ready to be enamelled. An interesting fact is that, although it is now pure silver, the

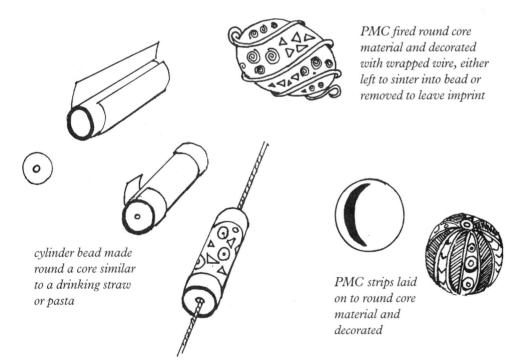

PMC fired round core material and decorated with wrapped wire, either left to sinter into bead or removed to leave imprint

cylinder bead made round a core similar to a drinking straw or pasta

PMC strips laid on to round core material and decorated

Variations in PMC bead shapes.

A bead within a bead. Core of papier mâché with a sintered bead (A) embedded in the centre. PMC round the papier mâché is decorated and fired.

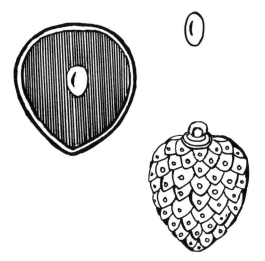

until it is about ten to twelve layers thick. Let the final form dry completely and sinter. As the fumes from wax can be rather noxious it is advisable to do this in a well-ventilated atmosphere. Experience is necessary to determine the depth of carving into the wax and the quality of detail required in a particular design, because the final silver form, although very strong, is too thin to allow any further refinement of the surface.

Another intriguing modification is to make a very small PMC bead and embed it in the centre of the core material; then, when the larger bead is sintered and the core material has burned away, the smaller bead is left free-moving inside. If the outer bead is made with strips to form a cage the inner bead will be visible, and this can be both decorative and melodic.

hollow PMC form is as strong as a hollow form made of standard silver.

It is possible to carve a pattern into the surface of a core made in wax and then take some slip and paint it on to the wax. Allow the slip to dry, then add more slip

Enamelled imprints of Yemeni architecture in PMC. Jeanne Werge-Hartley.

CLOISONS IN PMC

Cloisons can be made in PMC by rolling it out and cutting very thin short lengths with a scalpel and placing them on to a flat or curved surface of PMC. Once in place take a very fine paintbrush and, with water or slip, seal the edges of the cloisons to the base to stop them from lifting. Pure silver or hardenable cloisonné wire can be embedded in the PMC prior to firing. This can be very effective on beads and is a much more delicate approach for enamelling purposes. Hardenable silver wire does not need to be hardened before sintering as the silver will be hardened sufficiently in the sintering process. Pure gold, or a high-karat gold cloisonné wire could be used in a similar way with very thin hammered or rolled pieces of gold sheet embedded into the areas to be enamelled, enabling the red transparent enamel colours to be incorporated.

After trying out natural and found objects to texture the PMC, such as nets, mesh, leaves and stencilled paper, the next stage is to design and make personal punches and patterns to imprint it. These can be made by making negatives in metal, wood or plastic and, so long as the imprints are deep enough, they will retain enamel once the piece is sintered.

New products are appearing on the market and it is possible to purchase packs of thin sheet PMC and a syringe already prepared and filled with a thin PMC slip ready for use. Although the syringe appears to be expensive, it can be refilled with slip made from leftover scrap pieces, including those cut away at the 'leather' stage. (Such scraps should be covered in water and left in a container.) PMC3 is a new version that will fire at lower temperatures (see chart on page 148), has less shrinkage than PMC and PMC Plus, and is slightly more dense. Many designers prefer to use the standard PMC for the intricate detail, which the 28 per cent shrinkage allows. The combination of PMC, enamel, porcelain and other clays offers new and exciting potential for experienced designers.

Hairpin in hardenable silver, PMC and enamel. Jeanne Werge-Hartley.

Other Precious Metal Clays

Apart from silver and pure gold clays there are platinum and 18K golds, and yellow, white and pink golds. However, these are prohibitively expensive and their complex sintering is not possible in the average workshop.

157

10 HEALTH AND SAFETY

Enamelling, like many crafts, involves processes that have inherent dangers, and these dangers are increased when silversmithing and jewellery techniques are involved. Never eat, drink or smoke in the workshop, and always wear appropriate clothing and protection. While these serve as general rules, the use of acids, fluxes, enamels, fire and machinery all need additional stringent precautions if accidents are to be prevented.

ACIDS

General Rules for Working with Acids
• Always add acid slowly to purified water to prevent spitting and overheating. The solution will heat when mixed, so a heat-resistant container is needed such as a Pyrex bowl or a glass laboratory stoppered jar.
• Wear protective clothing, gloves and safety goggles when mixing acid.
• Always neutralize acid spills, drips or splashes with bicarbonate of soda.
• If you get any acid into your eyes wash your eye immediately and thoroughly with water and then with a solution of bicarbonate of soda before seeking medical attention.
• Use only brass or plastic tweezers in the acid as nickel or iron will contaminate it.
• The container should have a tight-fitting lid as the acid fumes are dangerous – not only harmful to breathe in but also ruinous to fabrics and materials in the vicinity.
• All hollow forms that have been in acid should be boiled out in an alkaline solution of bicarbonate or washing soda and then washed out thoroughly under warm running water.
• Always neutralize acids with an alkali before disposing of them. Large quantities should be dealt and disposed of by an authorized firm.
• Hydrofluoric acid for removing enamel: this is **not recommended in any situation,** as it needs full protective clothing, long rubber gloves and a high-specification fume cupboard for safe use.

Dilution of Cleaning Acids
Cleaning acids are used to remove surface oxides such as fused fluxes and carbonaceous deposits.
• Sulphuric acid (H_2SO_4) for silver: 10 parts pure water to 1 part acid.
• Sulphuric acid (H_2SO_4) for gold: 5–10 parts pure water to 1 part acid.
• Nitric acid (HNO_3) for gold: 20 parts pure water to 1 part acid.
• Sulphuric acid with potassium dichromate for white gold: 8.5 parts pure water to 1 part acid and 1.5 parts potassium dichromate.
• Hydrochloric acid (HC_l) for platinum: 8 parts pure water to 1–2 parts acid. Goggles must be worn when using this acid. A splash in the eye must be treated immediately, by washing the eye continuously until reaching hospital.
• Safety Pickle (proprietary brand name of Hoben Davis) for all metals: easier to use than sulphuric acid but still corrosive and not suitable for use with enamel.
• Alum (aluminium potassium sulphate): dissolve approximately 10g in 600ml of

water. Boil the metal in this solution until it is clean and then wash it in hot water. With this procedure there is no need for a hollow form to be boiled in bicarbonate of soda.

Dilution and Safe Handling of Etching Acids

• Nitric acid (HNO_3) for silver: 4 parts pure water to 1 part acid.
• Ferric nitrate for silver: 4 parts pure water to 1 part ferric nitrate. This comes in a crystalline form and gives a better etch than nitric acid in so far that it does not undercut. It stains the fingers and is corrosive, so wear protective gloves. It should be used at just above room temperature and kept covered as much as possible as it emits unpleasant fumes.
• Aqua Regis for gold and platinum: 3 parts sulphuric or hydrochloric acid to 1 part nitric acid. This is dangerous as heat is generated by the combination, so be sure to add one acid to the other very slowly.
• Ferric chloride for brass: 4 parts water to 1 part ferric chloride. This is used for stamping and roller printing. It comes in a crystalline form, and protective gloves should be used when mixing. Keep at room temperature and covered because it has unpleasant fumes.

Note that any acid will continue to etch once out of the solution even if immersed in water. To stop the etch totally you must brush the piece gently in a mix of warm, soapy water and ammonia.

SAFE WORKING WITH ENAMELS

• All British, French and Japanese enamels contain some lead and it is important to wash your hands after handling them. (This also applies to using a lead block when stamping, or when using it instead of pitch for small areas of repoussé.)
• Wear a mask when sifting enamels so that the fine powder is not inhaled.

SAFE WORKING WITH POLISHING MACHINES

Total concentration is vital when working on a polishing motor or a flexi-drive. Hold the piece you are polishing firmly in both hands but do not get your fingers entwined in the work. When polishing a chain, wrap it round a small block of soft wood and polish in sections. This prevents the chain from flying free and wrapping round the spindle.

Wear a mask so you do not inhale the polishing dust, especially the rouge polish,

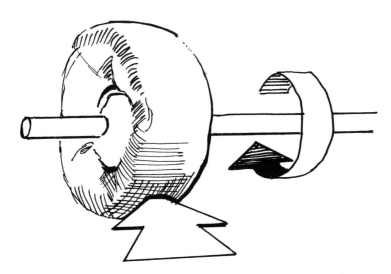

Using the lower quarter section of a polishing mop.

Brooch in hardenable silver, 18K gold, enamel, and textured PMC. 2002. Jeanne Wedge-Hartley.

and wear goggles to protect your eyes. Always tie back long hair and, if you have a longish fringe, wear a bandeau round your head, particularly if you are using the flexi-drive. Loose clothing needs to be secured. Never work close to the body and clothing with a flexi-drive. Only work on the lower quarter section of the polishing mop.

NB In the UK, workshops are required to have an extractor fan attached to the polishing motor.

Kaowool Ceramic Fibre (Product Reference CAS 65997-17-3)

Read the health and safety data sheet for this ceramic fibre, available from Vitrum Signum, and bear in mind the following general rules:

• Keep the product dry.
• Avoid generating dust when cutting or breaking.
• Wear goggles and gloves when handling larger quantities.
• Avoid tight collars and cuffs.
• Wear a suitable respirator when over-exposed to this material for a long time.

First Aid

• Skin contact – wash thoroughly with soap and water.
• Eyes – flood with water.
• Inhalation – remove from contact.

KILN SAFETY

Electric Shocks

Kilns should be fitted with a safety device that isolates the current from the elements when the door is open. Kilns with concealed elements are still a risk if cracks are evident in the walls or floor.

Gas Leaks

Gas leaks are possible from any joint or connection, particularly in flexible hoses. Examine them regularly and turn off at the main when not in use. A gas kiln should be fitted with a flame failure shut-off valve.

Eyes

Looking into a hot kiln may affect the eyes, so wearing protective goggles is advisable. Wearers of contact lenses should be aware that they may dry out in the heat.

BIBLIOGRAPHY

HISTORY

Becker, V., *The Jewellery of René Lalique* (The Goldsmiths' Company, 1998)
Gere, C. and Munn, G.C., A*rtists Jewellery* (Antique Collectors Club, 1989)
Nelson Dawson, Mrs E., *Enamels* (Methuen and Co., 1906)
Speel, E., *Dictionary of Enamelling* (Ashgate, 1998)

ENAMELLING TECH-NIQUES

Ball, F., *Experimental Techniques in Enamelling* (Van Nostrand Reinhold, 1972)
Bates, K., *Enamelling, Principles and Practice* (World Publishing Co.)
Fisher, A., *The Art of Enamelling upon Metal* (Studio)
Millenet, L. (trans. H. de Koningh), *Enamelling on Metal* (London Technical Press)
Seeler, M., *The Art of Enamelling* (Van Nostrand Reinhold, 1969)
Untracht, O., *Enamelling on Metal* (6th edn) (Isaac Pitman, 1958)

METAL TECHNIQUES

Edwardes, R., *Techniques of Jewellery* (B.T. Batsford Ltd, 1977)
Macrae, S., *Designing and Making Jewellery* (The Crowood Press, 2000)
McCreight, T., *The Complete Metalsmith* (Davis Publications Inc., 1991)
Untracht, O., *Jewellery, Concepts and Technology* (Hale, 1982)

PRECIOUS METAL CLAY

McCreight, T., *Working with Precious Metal Clay* (Brynmorgen Press, 2000)

JOURNALS

Crafts, Crafts Council, 44a Pentonville Road, London N1 9BY
Studio PMC, available from PO Box 257, Bennington, VT05201-0257, USA; or visit www.pmclay.com

TECHNICAL INFORMATION

ENAMEL COLOURS

(by kind permission of Vitrum Signum)

Blythe Enamels

800–840°C (1472–1544°F)		760–800°C (1400–1472°F)		720–760°C (1328–1400°F)	
L21 Kingfisher		A14 Rose Pink	(3050)	A26 Cherry Red	(3047)
M1 Mauve	(3053)	A21 Rich Ruby Red		A28 Light Red	(3049)
H3 Light Orange	(3031)	C1 Medium Flux	(139)	A31 Red	(3048)
H13 Orange Beige	(3032)	C10 Gold Flux		A34 Rose	
H20 Buttermilk		K6 Grass Green	(3073)	C2 Soft Flux	
L16 Powder Blue	(3006)	K16 Green	(3070)	K59 Olive Green	
N9 Pale Blue		K17 Almond Green	(3071)	K62 Grass Green	(3073)
N11 Pale Turquoise	(3000)	K39 Emerald Green	(3072)	L2 Mazarine Blue	(3074)
N15 Turquoise	(3003)	L27 Blue	(3077)	L5 Pearl Grey	
V12 Pale Grey	(3021)	L56 Sapphire		L12 Mid Blue	(49)
V15 Dark Grey	(3024)	M4 Pale Mauve	(3054)	L37 Deep Blue	
T8 Blossom		M9 Mauve	(3189)	L38 Light Blue	(3078)
		N14 Turquoise	(3079)	M8 Amethyst	
		N18 Aquarium		R2 Light Brown	(3060)
		N19 Turquoise		R5 Red Brown	(3059)
		N21 Celeste		V18 Misty Grey	
		R9 Dark Brown	(3054)	V23 Haematite	
		V2 Light Grey	(3068)	E1 Black	(3011)
		A12 Pink	(3043)	K18 Duck Egg Green	(3013)
		A24 Flesh Pink	(3042)	K31 Brunswick Green	(3016)
		A25 Mauve	(3040)	K60 Leaf Green	
		E5 Dense Black		P13 Terracotta	
		H11 Yellow	(3029)	P15 Scarlet	
		H19 Cream	(3027)	P16 Burnt Orange	
		H22 Marigold		P17 Sunflower	
		K13 Apple Green		P18 Red	
		K29 Longleat Green		P19 Post Office Red	
		K34 Lime Green	(3014)	P21 Deep Orange	
		K40 Meadow Green	(3017)	P22 Tangerine	
		K43 Dark Green	(3019)		
		L17 Mid Blue	(3007)		

L26 Lupin Blue (3005)
L52 Deep Blue
N4 Turquoise (0255)
N8 Sea Blue
N10 Forget Me Not (3001)
N23 Turquoise
R4 Ochre Brown (3034)
R8 Beech Brown (3037)
R16 Dark Brown
T6 Medium White (3025)
T7 White
V4 Pigeon Grey (3022)
V22 Silver Grey (3023)

Original Schauer Enamels

770–820°C (1418–1508°F)			*730–770°C (1346–1418°F)*			*700–730°C (1292–1346°F)*		
1401	Med Ruby Red	(ST16)	2A	Blue Flux	(ST17)	1W	Silver Flux	(ST3)
6023	Hard Flux	(ST4)	3	Yellow	(ST26)	28	Steel Blue	(ST38)
200	Hard White	(SOH)	6	Yellow Brown	(ST10)	109L	Light Brown	(ST9)
1627	Iris Blue	(opal)	8	Dk Ruby Red	(ST51)	111	Garnet	(ST15)
			19A	Lt Grassgreen	(ST29)	115	Med Ruby Red	(ST14)
			20A	Yellow Green	(ST28)	122	Grey	(ST25)
			26	Violet	(ST20)	128	Dk Grassgreen	(ST31)
			27	Light Violet	(ST19)	145	Olive Green	(ST27)
			43	Turq Blue	(ST33)	165	Medium Blue	(ST43)
			46	Dark Violet	(ST49)	171	Turquoise	(ST36)
			61	Turquoise	(ST34)	185	Medium Green	(ST32)
			84	Light Grey	(ST24)	186	Medium Green	(ST30)
			85	Rose	(ST12)	295T	Turquoise	(ST35)
			105	Golden Yellow	(ST6)	1619	Light Blue	(ST47)
			134	Blue	(ST39)	1710	Violet Grey	(ST18)
			138	Green Blue	(ST50)	6092	Grey	(ST23)
			154	Dark Blue	(ST45)	7042	Yellow	(ST7)
				Medium Blue	(ST41)	203	Soft White	(SO2)
			157	Light Blue	(ST46)	210A	Lemon	(SO5)
			174	Turq Blue	(ST37)	211	Yolk Yellow	(SO8)
			1380	Normal Flux	(ST2)	267	Turquoise	(SO35)
			5005	Ruby Red	(ST13)	294	Yellow	(SO7)
			5039	Dark Brown	(ST11)	314	Light Olive	(SO29)
			5275	Forget-Me-Not	(ST40)	345	Light Blue	(SO38)
			5424	Dark Blue	(ST44)	800	Light Blue	(SO37)
			6073	Blue	(ST42)	812	Turquoise	(SO36)
			6080	Violet	(ST22)	816	Lt Blue Green	(SO21)

6377	Orange	(ST8)	1101 Dk Blue Grey	(SO18)
6886	Yellow	(ST5)	1120 Medium Grey	(SO51)
6945	Violet	(ST21)	1132 Light Grey	(SO17)
201	Medium White	(SO1)	5247 Dk Blue Green	(SO28)
207	Ivory	(SO4)	6824 Light Green	(SO23)
214	Violet Grey	(SO49)	6960 Medium Blue	(SO41)
216	Grey	(SO50)	73 Blue	
220	Dark Grey	(SO19)		
225	Grassgreen	(SO26)	650–700°C (1202–1292°F)	
230	Dark Green	(SO27)	7551 Supersoft Flux	(ST1)
236	Light Green	(SO22)		
238	Parrot Green	(SO24)		
247	Medium Blue	(SO45)		
252	Medium Blue	(SO42)		
254	Dark Blue	(SO43)		
262	Lt Turquoise	(SO34)		
272	Violet	(SO31)		
285	Light Blue	(SO39)		
344	Dark Violet	(SO33)		
802	Light Blue	(SO40)		
811	Dk Heliotrope	(SO32)		
6013	Orange Red	(SO10)		
6284	Dark Brown	(SO16)		
6663	Bordeux Red	(SO13)		
6682	Yellow	(SO6)		
6800	Orange	(SO9)		
6805	Heraldic Red	(SO11)		
6813	Red	(SO12)		
6871	Ivory	(SO3)		
6857	Dk Red Brown	(SO15)		
6880	Leaf Green	(SO25)		
6890	Black	(SO46)		
6915	Brown	(SO14)		
6968	Yellow Green	(SO20)		
7142	Rose	(SO48)		
7143	Rose	(SO30)		
7148	Light Rose	(SO47)		
64	White			
75	Rose			
76	Rose			
77	Grey Green			
78	Turquoise			
80	Blue			
1658	Grey			
5735	Light Blue			
6969	Green			

Soyer Jewellery Enamels

Transparents

840–900°C (1544–1652°F)			800–840°C (1472–1544°F)			750–800°C (1382–1472°F)		
1	Copper Flux	(601)	2	Gold Flux	(602)	15	Pale Yellow	
10	Dark Green		3	Silver Flux	(603)	17	Light Yellow	
33	Pale Pink Lilac	(639)	4	Deep Blue		20	Bishops Purple	(638)
39	Mid Red		8	Dark Red		28	Pale Yellow Orange	
40	Light Red		13	Grey Blue		29	Pale Lilac	
41	Light Red		23	Mid Blue		32	Mid Brown	
45	Blue Turquoise		25	Mid Blue	(611)	172	Pale Yellow Brown	(622)
48	Mid Green		26	Deep Blue	(612)	191	Mid Purple	
49	Grassgreen	(606)	27	Deep Blue		518	Finishing Flux	
50	Deep Grassgreen	(607)	36	Black		619	Finishing Flux	
51	Deep Sea Green		38	Light Orange	(634)	1940	Pale Warm Pink	
52	Deep Grassgreen	(608)	46	Green Turquoise	(618)	1941	Pale Warm Pink	
53	Mid Purple		47	Rich Yellow		2000	Redcurrant	
119	Rich Grassgreen		100	Lavender		2002	Light Pink	(636)
174	Mid Brown		103	Deep Turquoise	(620)			
175	Dark Brown	(624)	104	Light Purple				
176	Deep Brown		111	Pale Lilac				
1943	Carnation Pink	(637)	161B	Grey Blue	(627)			
			163	Dark Blue	(613)			
			173	Light Brown	(623)			
			177	Black	(641)			
			184	Light Blue	(617)			
			185	Mid Turq Blue	(619)			
			186	Mid Turq Blue				
			188	Green				
			189	Mid Yellow Green	(609)			
			194	Dark Purple				
			238	Light Turq Blue				
			239	Light Turq Blue	(614)			
			240	Light Turq Green				
			241	Mid Grey Blue				
			250	Light Green	(621)			
			251	Mid Blue	(615)			
			256	Pale Yellow Green	(610)			
			600	Violet Grey				
			601	Green Grey	(628)			
			602	Earth Grey				
			603	Mouse Grey	(629)			
			604	Turquoise Grey	(630)			
			612	Madonna Blue				
			614	Light Brown				
			616	Pale Violet Blue				

1044 Rose
1942 Cyclamen Pink   (630)

Opaques

840–900°C (1544–1652°F)	*800–840°C (1472–1544°F)*	*750–800°C (1382–1472°F)*
81 Light Turquoise	71 Light Grey	59 White
82 Mid Turquoise	75 Light Yellow	62 Dark Blue
	76 Bright Yellow	66 Lavender
	83 Dark Green	68 Lavender
	91 Mid Yellow	74 Ivory
	254 Mid Turquoise	84 Mid Green
	297 Light Pink	88 Ivory
	298 Light Pink	97 Off White
	304 Old Grey	98 Off White
	306 Light Beige	148 White
	307 Mid Brown	157 Off White
		159 White
		160 White
		161 White
		195 Dark Blue
		196 Mid Blue
		200 Very Grey Pale Blue
		248 Light Green
		294 Mid Red
		295 Bright Red
		430 Mid Lilac
		490 Mid Orange
		491 Bright Orange
		605 Dark Sea Blue
		606 Moss Green
		625 S. Soft White (740°C)

Opalescents

750–800°C (1382–1472°F)

101 Opal White 800
607 Opal Rose   801
608 Opal Blue   802
609 Opal Yellow 803
610 Opal Green 804

USING RED ENAMELS

(by kind permission of Vitrum Signum)

Metal Preparation

These enamels are designed for use on silver or gold (14–24K), which has been degreased and deoxidized mechanically or chemically, as appropriate, immediately prior to use.

Enamel Preparation

The transparents attain greatest clarity and the opaques greatest colour density after rinsing well in purified water just prior to use.

Blythe Enamels

For application on silver the following 'gold-bearing' transparent and opalescent colours should be fired over a base coat of C1 Medium Flux (139).
Recommended firing temperature: 730–820°C (1346–1508°F)

A14	Rose Pink	(3050)
A21	Rich Ruby Red	
A26	Cherry Red	(3047)
A28	Light Red	(3049)
A31	Red	(3048)
A34	Rose	

The opalescent T8 Blossom is suitable for use over silver with C1 Flux.

Original Schauer Enamels

For application on silver, the following 'gold-bearing' transparent and opalescent colours should be fired over a base coat of 2A Blue Flux (ST17).
Recommended firing temperature: 730–820°C (1346–1508°F)

8	Dark Ruby Red	(ST51)
85	Rose	(ST12)
111	Garnet	(ST15)
115	Medium Ruby Red	(ST14)
1401	Medium Ruby Red	(ST16)
5005	Ruby Red	(ST13)
75	Rose	
76	Rose	

Soyer Enamels

For application on silver, the following 'gold-bearing' transparent colours should be fired over a base coat of SOJE3 Silver Flux (603).
Recommended firing temperature: 750–900°C (1382–1652°F)

8	Dark Red	
20	Bishops Purple	(638)
39	Mid Red	

40	Light Red	
41	Light Red	
1044	Rose	
1940	Pale Warm Pink	
1941	Pale Warm Pink	
1942	Cyclamen Pink	(630)
1943	Carnation Pink	(637)
2000	Redcurrant	
2002	Light Pink	(636)

Original Latham and British Professional Enamels

For application on silver the following 'gold-bearing' transparent enamels should be fired over a base coat of 6426 Hard Silver Flux.

Recommended firing temperature: 750–900°C (1382–1652°F)

T201	Light Rose	(6407)
T202	Rose	(6229)
T203	Ruby	(6223)
T236	Cherry Red	(6228)
T239	Deep Ruby	(6210)
T240	Blue Ruby	(6424)
T247	Blue Rose	(6447)
T248	Dusty Rose	(6448)
T249	Nectarine	(6449)
T251	Garnet	(6454)

Japanese Kujaku Jewellery Enamels

KJE	transparent.
105A	Ruby Red
105B	Rich Ruby Red

MELTING POINTS OF SOLDERS

Solder	°C	°F
Platinum extra easy	935–955	1718–1750
Platinum easy	1010–1030	1850–1886
Gold 9K white	725–735	1335–1355
Gold 14K easy	710–730	1310–1346
Gold 14K hard	750–785	1382–1445
Yellow gold 18K easy	700–715	1292–1320
Yellow gold 18K med	730–765	1346–1410
Yellow gold 18K hard	790–830	1454–1526
White gold 18K easy	690–710	1274–1310
White gold 18K med	705–720	1300–1328
White gold 18K hard	855–885	1572–1625
White gold 18K Xhard	835–885	1535–1625
Red gold 18K easy	730–805	1346–1480
Red gold 18K med	805–810	1480–1490
Red gold 18K hard	750–840	1382–1544
Gold 22K	865–900	1590–1652
Silver Il enamel	730–800	1346–1472
Silver/zinc hard	745–780	1376–1436
Silver H4 med	720–765	1328–1410
Silver 96 easy	705–725	1300–1338
Silver 96 X easy	665–710	1230–1310

USEFUL ADDRESSES

SUPPLIERS

UK

Cooksons Precious Metals Ltd
Vittoria Street
Birmingham B1 3NZ
www.cooksongold.com
For precious metals.

Cookson Exchange Findings
49 Hatton Garden
London EC1N 8YS
www.exchangefindings.com
For jewellery tools, precious metals and
findings, micro-weld equipment.

Eagle Electrical Engineers
Eagle House
Coney Lane
Keighley BD21 5JE
Tel: +44 (0) 1535 606331
Fax: +44 (0) 1535 606332
email: sales@eagle-elec.co.uk
For kiln control units.

Euro Findings
Minerva House
26–27 Hatton Garden
London EC1N 8BR
Tel: +44 (0) 20 7404 5762
Fax: +44 (0) 20 7831 6701
For jewellery tools.

Fred Aldous Ltd
37 Lever Street
Manchester M60 1UX
www.fredaldous.co.uk
For art and craft supplies and kilns.

Guill and Stevenson
Penny Bank Chambers
33–35 St John's Square
London EC1N 4DN
Tel: +44 (0) 20 7250 6651
Engraving undertaken.

H.S. Walsh & Sons Ltd
Head Office
243 Beckenham Road
Beckenham BR3 4TS
email: hswalsh@dial.pipex.com
For jewellery tools, kilns, polishing motors
and flexi-drives.

Birmingham Branch
1–2 Warstone Mews
Warstone Lane
Birmingham B18 6JB

London Branch
21 St Cross Street
Hatton Garden
London EC1N 8UN

Hadleigh Enterprises Ltd
533 Rayleigh Road
Thundersly
Benfleet SS7 3TR
Tel: +44 (0) 1268 572255
For polyester silicone tape (acid-resist
tape 23mm × 33m).

J. Blundell & Sons Ltd
31–35 Leather Lane
London EC1N 7JE
Tel: +44 (0) 207 404 0744/685
Fax: +44 (0) 207 242 3133
email: jblundell@fabdial.co.uk
For precious metals, jewellery tools
and findings.

L. Cornelissen and Son Ltd
105 Great Russell Street
London WC1B 3RY
Tel: +44 (0) 20 7636 1045
Fax: +44 (0) 20 7636 3655
For all etching equipment, including a
large selection of burnishers. Worldwide
mail order service available.

Maplin Electronics
Branches throughout the UK.
Supplies photo-resist materials, electrolube
positive photo-resist spray, electrolube
photo-resist developer and stopping-out
pens (Decon, Dalo, 33 Blue).

Marcia Lanyon
PO Box 370
London W6 7ED
Tel: +44 (0) 20 7602 2446
Fax: +44 (0) 20 7602 0382
email: sales@marcialanyon.com
For gemstones and beads.

Micro Metallic Ltd
70 Woodside Business Park
Shore Road
Birkenhead L41 1EH
Tel: +44 (0) 151 647 4641
For industrial photo-etching.

Milton Bridge Ceramic Colours Ltd
Unit 9, Trent Trading Park
Botteslow Street
Hanley
Stoke-on-Trent ST1 3NA
Tel: +44 (0) 1782 274229
Fax: +44 (0) 1782 281591
For enamels and kilns.

Northern Kilns
Pilling Pottery
School Lane
Pilling
Nr Garstang PR3 6HB
Tel: +44 (0) 1253 790307
Fax: +44 (0) 1253 790120

For new and reconditioned kilns from
stock or made to order. Spares and shelves
cut to size.

Rashbell Marketing, UK
24–28 Hatton Wall
London EC1N 8JH
Tel: +44 (0) 20 7831 5646
www.rashbell.com
Precious metals, findings and tools.

Stewart R. Stevenson
68 Clerkenwell Road
London EC1N 5QA
Tel: +44 (0) 20 7253 1693
For silver and gold foil in various
thicknesses.

Surechem Products Ltd
Lion Barn Industrial Estate
Needham Market IP6 8NZ
email: sales@surechem.co.uk
www.surechem.co.uk
For ferric chloride and ferric nitrate.
Supplied to business addresses only.

The Goldsmith's Company Directory
www.whoswhoingoldandsilver.com

Thomas Sutton Tools
37 Frederick Street
Birmingham B1 3HN
Tel: +44 (0) 121 236 7139
Fax: +44 (0) 121 236 4318
For all jewellery and silversmithing tools.

Vitrum Signum
www.vitrumsignum.co.uk
All enamels, kilns, etc.

W.G. Ball Ltd
Dept G Anchor Road
Longton
Stoke-on-Trent ST3 1JW
Tel: +44 (0) 1782 313956/313386
Fax: +44 (0) 1782 598148
For lead-free enamels.

PHOTOETCHING
Chempix
PO Box 16230
Curzon St
Birmingham B4 7XD
www.chempix.com

ENGRAVING
Guill and Stephenson
Penny Bank Chambers
33–35 St John's Square
London EC1N 4DN
Tel. + 44(0) 20 725 13667

USA
Allcraft
135 West 29th Street
Suite 402
New York
NY 10001
USA
Tel: 001 800 645 7124 (order hotline)
Fax: 001 800 645 7125
For tools and supplies.

Metalliferous Inc.
34 West 46th Street
New York
NY 10036
USA
Tel: 001 212 944 0909
Fax: 001 212 944 0644
For tools, micron abrasive finishing
sheets, fancy tubes, rods, patterned
sheets and far more. Worldwide mail
order service available.

Rio Grande
7500 Bluewater Road
Albuquerque
NM 87121
USA
www.riogrande.com
For Precious Metal Clay, tools, materi-
als and micron abrasive finishing sheets.
This firm has an excellent catalogue and
runs a worldwide mail order service.

Thompson Enamels
PO Box 310
Newport
KY 41072
USA
Tel: 001 606 291 3800
Fax: 001 606 291 1849

Japan
Kujaku Enamels
Aoki Metals Ltd
25-1 Narimasu 3-Chome
Itabashi–Ku
Tokyo 175
Japan
Tel: +81 (0) 3 3930 1192
For enamels.

Mitsubishi Material Materials
Ofs West 20F
1-5-1 Ohtemachi
Chiyoda-Ku
Tokyo 100-8117
Japan
Tel: +81 (0) 3 5252 5430
Fax: +81 (0) 3 5252 5442
For Precious Metal Clay.

Ninomiya Color Shippo Co. Ltd
3-10-19 Shirahata
Saitama – City
Saitama – Pre
Japan 336-0022
email: lumuse2@yahoo.co.jp
For enamels (price list supplied).

ORGANIZATIONS

**Association for Contemporary
Jewellery**
PO Box 37807
London SE23 1XJ
www.acj.org.uk

British Society of Enamellers
www.cidae.com

The Crafts Council
44a Pentonville Road
Islington
London N1 9BY
www.craftscouncil.org.uk

Designer Jewellers Group
24 Rivington Street
London EC2A 3DU
www.designerjewellersgroup.co.uk

Edward James Foundation
West Dean College
West Dean
Nr Chichester
PO18 0QZ
email: westdean@pavilion.co.uk
www.westdean.org.uk

Guild of Enamellers
Contact Shirley Gore
s.gore12@ntworld.com

Society of Designer Craftsmen
24 Rivington Street
London EC2A 3DU
email: secretary@societydesigncraft.org.uk

Studio Fusion
Oxo Tower Wharfe
Bargehouse Street
South Bank
London SE1 9PH
Tel: +44 (0) 20 7928 3600
www.oxotower.co.uk

Tadema Gallery
10 Charlton Place
Camden Passage
London N1 8AJ
Tel: +44 (0) 20 7359 1053

The Worshipful Company of Goldsmiths
Goldsmiths' Hall
Foster Lane
London EC2V 6BN
www.thegoldsmiths.co.uk

INDEX

6/11